101

Little Known Facts

With Dale Robertson

101
Little Known Facts

With Dale Robertson

Chaz Allen

CITADEL PRESS
Kensington Publishing Corp.
www.kensingtonbooks.com

To my friend Dale Robertson.
The greatest cowboy and actor,
I have ever known.

CITADEL PRESS BOOKS are published by

Kensington Publishing Corp.
850 Third Avenue
New York, NY 10022

All Kensington titles, imprints, and distributed lines are available at special quantity discounts for bulk purchases for sales promotions, premiums, fund-raising, educational, or institutional use. Special book excerpts or customized printings can also be created to fit specific needs. For details, write or phone the office of the Kensington special sales manager: Kensington Publishing Corp., 850 Third Avenue, New York, NY 10022, attn: Special Sales Department, phone 1-800-221-2647.

Citadel Press and the Citadel Logo are trademarks of Kensington Publishing Corp.

Design by Leonard Telesca

First printing: May 2002

10 9 8 7 6 5 4 3 2 1

Printed in the United States of America

Library of Congress Control Number: 2001099892

ISBN: 0-8065-2339-5

Contents

Acknowledgments

I wish to extend my very special gratitude to Michael Steelman M.D., Joyce Moseley, Mike and Patsy Burdine, Phil and Jane Isaac, Jane Tomlinson and Curt and Janis Munson for their enormous contribution to this work.

Chaz Allen

LITTLE-KNOWN FACT #1

It's Greek to Me

You parents know that there's one question that kids will always ask when you're on the road. And that is, of course: Are we there yet? Well, there's another question the youngsters will always ask the first time you drive into San Francisco. We'll get to that in just a minute.

But first, let's talk about the amazing career of one Captain John Frémont. John was born in Savannah, Georgia, in 1813, but in no time at all, he realized that his future waited for him in the wild and unexplored western United States.

He explored some areas of the West, especially in California, where Europeans had never been before. He sent enthusiastic reports of his discoveries back East. Why, John Frémont made this western country so exciting that thousands of folks were catching the next wagon west.

Now, John didn't spend all his time in the West. After he joined the army, it was Captain John Frémont who sailed to most of the exotic ports around the world. One place that especially fascinated him was the harbor that led to the town of Istanbul. The people there called the harbor Chry-so-ceras. It was a name he never forgot.

Well, now, Captain John Frémont eventually returned to the Wild West of America that he loved so much. He continued his explorations until around 1846, when the people who had moved to California from the East started a revolt against the Mexican government, which owned California at the time.

Frémont led the fight against the Mexican army, which had been sent to control the rebellious immigrants. The Americans won the war and John was elected the first U.S. senator from California.

Not only did he help make California possible, but, like most explorers of the day, he was responsible for naming quite a few places in the new state. One of the things John named was the entrance to San Francisco Bay—a natural strait that is three miles long by one mile wide. He named the strait Chry-so-pylae, which is pretty close to the name of that harbor he loved so much back in Istanbul.

Now. What was that question the kids will always ask when you drive into San Franciso? Hey, Daddy, how come the bridge is orange?

It's a little-known fact that the name of America's most famous bridge refers to the strait of water underneath it, not to the bridge itself. You see, *chry-so-pylae*, in Greek, means "golden gate."

LITTLE-KNOWN FACT #2

A Tomboy's Tale

I probably don't have to remind anyone that women in the 1850s and 1860s didn't have the same opportunities as men. And I guess in some places, they still don't. But if you were a young woman back then and not satisfied with the traditional roles you were offered, then you might have to take some drastic action. Well, you know some women did then just what some do today—they protest and whine about it. But others take action. They don't just sit around and make talk and write a few protest letters, they go out and get what they want from life.

That was the case with Martha Jane. She was something of a free spirit, to say the least. She was almost always offended by the gender barriers that society put up, and she was always fighting them. But her way of fighting was to go and prove that she could do it. Martha Jane was something of a tomboy to begin with. She could ride a horse as well as almost any man, and was a crack shot with a Remington rifle, too. That was her favorite, the Remington.

When Martha found out that the transcontinental railroad was hiring and that they were paying some of the highest wages in the territory, she decided that she wanted that job. It was hard, backbreaking work, but no matter. What did matter is that the only job they offered her was as a cook or doing laundry for the men. Oh no! Not Martha. She decided that it was time for a little chicanery. She disguised herself as a man and went and applied for the job. And they hired her. For several weeks she worked right along with the men, shoulder to shoulder. No one was the wiser. Everyone thought that Martha was Marty! Just a baby-faced boy, but one who could work as hard as any of them.

No telling how long this would have gone on, except for a small incident that happened on a very hot afternoon. The men had been working laying rail for several hours. The afternoon temperature had to be in the nineties. It was a scorcher. The path of the tracks took them right by a lovely cool mountain lake. Needless to say, all the men stripped off their clothes and jumped in. Martha said later that she wasn't really sure what she was think-ing, except the lure of that cool water was more than she could resist. Yep! It's true, she stripped to her birthday suit and jumped in the water. It raised more than a few eye-brows. She was discovered and they fired her. Silly, isn't it? She had been doing the same work as the men for weeks. But that was the rule. She was out of there. All be-cause of a brief lapse in judgment and an irresistible cool mountain lake.

But that was what most of Martha's life consisted of . . . lapses in judgment of one kind or another, or just out-and-out lying. She had more than one embarrassing moment in her life and told more than one whopper of a tale. That's pretty much how she got her name. No, not Martha Jane—that's the one her parents gave her. I'm talking about the one that Wild Bill Hickok gave her. It's a little-known fact that Martha Jane Cannary, the woman who disguised her-self to work as a man and who was so prone to errors of judgment, became known for just that . . . calamities. She was Calamity Jane!

LITTLE-KNOWN FACT #3

Life Is a Gift

Anna was born in the mountains of upstate New York way back in 1860—one of ten children born to farmer Russell Robertson and his wife, Margaret. The Robertsons were poor. Formal education was considered a luxury. So Anna left home at the age of twelve and went to work for other families—cooking, cleaning, ironing, gardening, and taking care of the sick. At seventeen, she married Tom Man, who, like her father, was a hired man on a farm. Like her mother, she bore her husband ten children, though only five of them survived.

It would be nice to think that life got easier for Anna after she married Tom . . . but the truth is, it didn't. It seemed that backbreaking work was Anna's destiny. Even her honeymoon was a trip she and her husband took to North Carolina because they were supposed to begin work there as caretakers of a horse ranch. But that fell through, so Anna and Tom found work on a dairy farm instead. In addition to bearing and taking care of children and a home, Anna did farm chores including hand-churning as much as 160 pounds of butter a week. She was creative in finding ways to help put food on the table. And when her husband Tom passed away after forty years of marriage, she took over running the farm, too. After all, somebody needed to do it, and it's not as if hard work was anything new to Anna.

Reading this story, you might be thinking that Anna had an unhappy life. But you'd be wrong. Anna felt true joy in living and she shared it wherever she went. She also had a deep appreciation of beauty, so when she got too old to run the farm she took up needlework. But she didn't slack off on her cooking and canning. Her canned fruits and jam often brought prizes from the judges at the local fair. Anna worked at her needlecraft until her arthritis got so bad she had to quit. This was a hard pill to swallow for one so accustomed to hard work.

Anna just wasn't the rocking-chair type.

So at the age of seventy-eight, she picked up a paintbrush and decided to put some of that beauty that she had been seeing and feeling her whole life on canvas. And it's a little-known fact that had it not been for her arthritis, Anna Robertson Moses might never have picked up a brush, and Grandma Moses would have died without painting a single stroke.

LITTLE-KNOWN FACT #4

Arthur's Boy

I guess you'd have to call Arthur a true-blue soldier. When he earned the Congressional Medal of Honor during the Civil War, he was just eighteen years old. And before his career in the army was over, he'd served in many a ruckus. Why, he'd even been stationed for a time in New Mexico, where he fought Geronimo to tame the Wild West.

It so happens that Arthur had a son. And you can just imagine how proud he was when that boy decided to follow in his dad's footsteps . . . and become a soldier. Now, as good a soldier as Arthur was, his son was an even better one. During World War I he commanded his own division. And the way he inspired his men by fighting right alongside them . . . well, people still talk about it.

If you're up on your history, you know that it wasn't long after the end of World War I that we faced another kind of crisis. The Great Depression. You've surely heard older folks talk about how hard those times were. It worried Americans sick for ten long years. Well, after the war, Art's son was stationed for a time in Washington, D.C. And that was just his own plain bad luck. Because any army man can tell you that his commander in chief is the president of the United States . . . and that was Herbert Hoover.

Right or wrong, the American people held the president personally responsible for the Depression. And poor old H. H., well it must have seemed like he couldn't do anything right. Americans took to calling the shantytowns filled with poor folks Hoovervilles. When people had to shoot a rabbit just to have something to eat, they referred to their catch as a Hoover hog. And the shoes with holes in the soles that everybody seemed to be wearing those days—well, those were Hoover shoes. I'd say there couldn't have been a worse job than working for President Hoover. It sure got Arthur's boy into some hot water.

You see, in 1932, things were so bad for some World War I veterans that fifteen thousand of them decided to march on the nation's capital and demand early payment for some bonus pay certificates they'd earned in the war. When the senate said they couldn't afford to pay off on those bonuses until they were fully matured, a good many of those veterans went on back home. But some stayed in town, living in their own Hooverville of shacks alongside the river. I guess they figured it was as good a place as any to be broke and out of work. But finally President Hoover had enough and ordered them gone. Or else.

So in July of that year, the army used tanks, bayonets, and tear gas to clear them out. Now, it's a little-known fact that when the army rousted out those World War I veterans, the people in this country were spitting mad, especially at the man who led those troops. And as you've probably guessed, that poor soul was Arthur's boy. Or you might know him a little better by his own name . . . General Douglas MacArthur.

LITTLE-KNOWN FACT #5

The Baby Food Kid

If you weren't there, then it's hard to imagine just how tough things really were during the Depression. At least fifteen million people were out of work . . . thirty-two thousand businesses shut down for good . . . and five thousand banks went belly-up. In those days, banks were the common enemy; they had a miserable public image. When a bank went bust, families lost their life savings. Sometimes . . . the only way a bank could stay afloat was to foreclose on people's homes and farms. It's not all that surprising that Americans sometimes rooted for the bank robbers. Criminals were a whole lot more popular than bank presidents.

John Dillinger and his gang were famous! Americans followed their exploits like they would a running television series. The Dillinger gang was especially famous for destroying mortgage records of the banks they robbed. And as you might guess, it wasn't long before Hollywood caught on, and bank robbers and gangsters became a common sight on the big screen.

A long list of Hollywood movie stars got their big break that way: Edward G. Robinson, James Cagney, Kirk Douglas, and Robert Mitchum all got their start playing somebody on the wrong side of the law. But probably no one was better at it than Bogie. Humphrey Bogart. When he first hit the big screen in 1936, he specialized in acting like a bank robber. Or a gangster. Or an escaped convict. He played them so well that even convicted criminals serving out prison sentences were convinced that he was one of them. Inmates sent him piles of fan mail. Even when Bogie started getting a few plum roles, he never lost his gangster edge. His gruff, grizzled exterior spoke for itself.

But Humphrey Bogart was famous a whole lot of years before he made it big as a bad guy in the movies. And, well, he was anything but tough. "There was a time in American history," Bogie once said, "where you couldn't pick up a magazine without seeing my kisser..." but most people just didn't know it. It's a little-known fact that if you had bought a jar of Mellin baby food back at the turn of the twentieth century, it was his face you'd see on the front of the jar. It was his face that graced the magazine ads and billboards. And so it was that when America first came to know Humphrey Bogart, it wasn't as a bad guy, but rather in diapers.

LITTLE-KNOWN FACT #6

The Lousy Shot

He couldn't believe he was still alive. The enemy soldier had just fired five rounds from less than twenty feet away—and missed. Benjamin Kubelsky stood there dumbfounded. He kept checking himself for bullet holes. Well, at least he didn't have to worry about his mother getting that dreaded telegram telling her that her son had been shot or killed. Like most mothers, Ben's had been fretting about that ever since he joined the navy. She really didn't understand why Ben had to go off to war in the first place. This was something between the kaiser and a few French and she guessed the Brits got involved, too. Seemed like those Brits were always involved.

But why Ben? Why did he have to go? All her life the only thing she wanted was for her son to be a concert violinist. She spent almost every dime she had to see that he had lessons from the best teacher in town. But Ben seemed to fight the whole idea.

As a matter of fact, for a budding violin player, Ben was something of a rogue. He was thrown out of high school after only one year for bad behavior. And they wouldn't let him back in either. He tried several other jobs, all ending the same way school had. Finally his father decided that he would teach him haberdashery. At least as a hat maker, Ben could earn a living. And in 1915, nearly everyone wore a hat . . . so it was a good profession, one with a future.

But Ben didn't think much of that idea either. And when war broke out in Europe . . . he joined the navy. And now this!

He had been walking along with several of his buddies when a German soldier jumped from the side of the road and fired several shots at Ben at near point-blank range. And he missed. When they tackled the German, the man was nearly in tears, explaining that he was the worst shot in his regiment. As a matter of fact, he was so bad the others had left him behind. He was hoping that by shooting at such a close range, he could hit something and get back in the good graces of his commander. But no such luck. At least not for the German soldier.

But it sure was lucky for Ben . . . and for us. You see, it's a little-known fact that Benjamin Kubelsky ran into the worst shot in the German army—and it's a good thing he did, or we would have missed fifty years with one of the

funniest men in the whole world . . . the hilarious Jack
Benny!

LITTLE-KNOWN FACT #7

Thanks, Ben!

Benjamin was born in 1731, the son of a slave. He took a
last name from the place his grandfather had come from.
A place in Africa named Banna Ka.

Benjamin learned to read from his grandmother's Bible.
That and the fact that a Quaker schoolteacher set up a
school in the Virginia valley where he lived and taught
Benjamin to write and do simple arithmetic. Well, when
Benjamin was twenty-one, a friend showed him a pocket
watch. He was so fascinated by it that his friend gave it to
him and Benjamin took it apart to see how it worked. He
carved copies of the pieces out of wood and made a clock
of his own. Believe it or not, it was the first striking clock
made completely in America—but even more amazing, so
intricate and fine were its carving and craftsmanship that
it struck every hour for forty years.

Well, Ben found a profession in that hobby, and he went
on to repair watches and clocks and even helped famed
clockmaker Joseph Ellicot build a more complex clock.
Ellicott, in turn, gave Ben more books on the sciences.
Now Ben's interests were really piqued. He went on to
teach himself astronomy and advanced mathematics. He
even built himself a crude observatory.

The result was *Benjamin Banneker's Almanac*, first published in 1792. He was in correspondence with some of the

leading minds of the day, even writing to Thomas Jefferson. Ben impressed Jefferson, so it wasn't entirely out of the blue that Jefferson should make sure that Ben was named to the survey team when the new capital, Washington, D.C., was in its earliest planning stages. It was a lucky thing, too, make no mistake, for what happened next changed the course of history.

Ben worked closely with a Frenchman, Pierre L'Enfant, the architect in charge of planning Washington, D.C. But Pierre L'Enfant was not an easy man to deal with. He had a temper. Seems he alienated almost everyone he worked with. Because of that temper, he was suddenly dismissed from the project to design the nation's capital. To make matters worse, he left in a huff and took all the plans with him—a whole year of work now seemingly down the drain. Except for a brilliant man named Ben.

It's a little-known fact that we owe the design of our nation's capital to the son of a slave, because in two days, Benjamin Banneker re-created L'Enfant's designs entirely from memory. You might want to think about that next time you see a picture of our nation's capital, and say . . . thanks, Ben!

LITTLE-KNOWN FACT #8

The Village Smithy

It's hard to imagine now just how important the town blacksmith was to a farming community in the pioneer days. We don't use the services of a blacksmith anymore, but back then the blacksmith kept the stages and buckboards running . . . shod horses . . . even fixed your plow and hand tools. No, you couldn't do without the town blacksmith.

And so it was in the little farming village of Middlebury, Vermont, in 1825. That year, a young blacksmith named John came to the end of his apprenticeship and set out to find himself a job. He'd made good a name for himself as a blacksmith—people would come from miles around to ask for John in particular. In fact, folks often remarked that old tools left John's forge in better shape than when they were new.

Despite his fine reputation he ran through a series of blacksmithing jobs in his youth. He thought being his own boss might be the answer—and so he found himself a silent partner, a local fellow named Jay Wright. And he borrowed a substantial sum of money from investors. His neighbors pitched in to help him get established, and before long John's new blacksmith shop was up and running.

But John's dream was not to be, not just yet. One winter night, fire took the new blacksmith shop. And Jay proved that he was the right partner to have. He came to the rescue: John rebuilt. He opened a second shop and seemed to be on his way. But one disaster followed another and John's second shop was struck by lightning—and again he borrowed.

A third shop followed. But though John was spared any natural disaster this time, his fine workmanship couldn't save him from mounting debt. In 1836—with creditors, including Jay Wright, taking court action, and prison looming on the horizon—John sold out the shop and joined the thousands of Americans heading west.

John continued west till he reached the farming community of Grand Detour, Illinois. John had never seen anything like it. The soil was so rich, a far cry from the thin, rocky soil he'd left behind. This was the best farmland in the country—maybe in the world, he thought.

John went to set up shop and went to work. The farmers swarmed to the forge, eager to repair the tools that had gone unmended for so long. John was surprised to learn that the local men were dreading the chore of spring planting. Back east, planting was one of the better times of the farmers' year—full of promise despite the too-poor soil of northern New England. But here every farmer had the same complaint. That same rich, black soil that promised bountiful harvests was like glue—it would stick to the plow and make the going hard indeed.

John saw opportunity here. He experimented with a broken sawblade of Sheffield steel . . . a metal that was so slick, dirt didn't stick to it. What emerged was the first and only plow that could cut like a knife through that rich sticky soil—and come out clean. It revolutionized the plow and farming.

You might guess that John's invention was a hit, and it led to many many other farm products and a vital and growing industry that's a hallmark of dependability today. It's a little-known fact that the man who revolutionized the plow and made it possible to farm America's richest land was a blacksmith on the run from debts back home—think about that the next time you see a John Deere going across a field.

LITTLE-KNOWN FACT #9

Great Balls of Fire!

I bet you can still remember when a whole lot of Yellowstone Park and parts of north and west America burned to the ground. It wasn't that long ago that almost half of Yellowstone was scorched to a cinder. California lost a chunk of forest almost equal to Rhode Island. Yellowstone officials told us it would be years before the park was fully recovered . . . that it would take a whole generation to get it back to what it had been. We've seen our share of forest fires, but historians tell us that we'd have to look as far back as the 1600s to find this much charred terrain.

Of course, the cost of those 1988 fires was pretty steep. It took millions of dollars just to try to control all the damage. Why, if we'd been at war, there's no telling what would have happened. At least thirty thousand firefighters fought to put those fires out. And that's not counting all the military units called up to battle fifty-foot walls of flame. I guess it looked like the whole country was burning out that way. And a good number of our citizens were trying to put it out. But no matter what we did, those fires kept right on burning. That was one job only Mother Nature was big enough to handle. The flames didn't start to smolder until the first snows of September.

Those fires were a deadly enemy. And that's just the sort of situation the Japanese were hoping to create back in World War II. Near the end of the war, the Japanese launched nine thousand balloon bombs, hoping they'd travel six thousand miles across the Pacific to North America and set the United States on fire. Luckily for us, most of them went down somewhere over the Pacific, but at least 285 hit North American targets, most of them in the U.S. Northwest. Some even got as far east as Michigan. On May 5, 1945, five children and their Sunday school teacher were out picnicking in the woods and became the first and only casualties of that Japanese campaign. But those balloon bombs weren't the only attack the Japanese made on the U.S. mainland.

No sir, it's a little-known fact that in September 1942, a Japanese pilot flew over Mount Emily, Oregon, and dropped a bomb that was supposed to set the woods ablaze. Three weeks later, a Japanese plane bombed Port Orford, Oregon. The Japanese were so good at it that it wasn't until after the war that we even knew exactly what happened. And so the idea that the mainland U.S. has never been bombed by a foreign power, well, that went up in smoke. Right along with a few trees in Oregon.

LITTLE-KNOWN FACT #10

Her Daddy's Girl

Heavyweight fighters have always attracted a crowd and big money. Why, today a championship match can gross over a hundred million dollars. The fighters themselves get upwards of twenty or thirty million. Just for one fight. Seems like a lot of money, doesn't it? But the truth is that darn few of us are willing to do what those fellas do to make that money. Some of you don't know that Dale did a little prizefighting himself, before he got in the movie business . . . and he'll have to admit, he likes the movies better. But that doesn't change the fact that prizefighters make good money and sometimes become very famous.

Take Joe Louis, or Rocky Marciano, or John L. Sullivan. Now, it's been over seventy years since Sullivan fought, but most of you have heard his name. And he was a bare-knuckles champion, too. That means they didn't use gloves. Talk about tough hombres! John was scheduled to fight a fella by the name of Battlin' Jack one evening. The fight was well promoted and the men not only knew each other but were friends. Which is why what happened next is so interesting.

You see, Jack had a little daughter, Mary Jane. She was seven at the time. She knew her daddy worked at a boxing gym and even saw him spar a few times. This night, Mary Jane begged to go to the match. Jack was against it, but he couldn't find a baby-sitter, so he agreed, as long as Mary Jane agreed to behave herself. He sat her in the front row and the fight began. Battlin' Jack was pretty good, but no real match for world-champion Sullivan. Jack was getting knocked around pretty good.

When a cut opened over his eye, and blood started running down his face, he worried about how this might affect little Mary Jane. He didn't have to wonder long. She flew out of her seat in the middle of the fight, grabbed Sullivan's leg, and started biting it. Sullivan was in shock and pain all at the same time. Sullivan didn't want to hurt the child, but he didn't want to be bitten either. The referee and Mary Jane's father both tried to loosen her locked jaw on the champ, but her teeth were set. Finally, in frustration, Sullivan lay down on the canvas and pretended to be out cold. That did it! The child let go.

Well, it's a little-known fact that the world's bare-knuckles heavyweight champ was taken down by a seven-year-old girl. And that's really surprising when you realize that she probably became the world's model of feminine behavior a few years later. You see, she was Battlin' Jack West's daughter all right . . . and they just called her Mae . . . Mae West.

LITTLE-KNOWN FACT #11

The Brooklyn Bridge?

I'll bet it's been sold to more suckers than anything else in the world. You've heard the old adage, "If you believe that, I've got a bridge I'd like to sell you"? Of course, I'm talking about the famed Brooklyn Bridge, which spans the East River from Manhattan to Brooklyn in New York City. It was one of the first suspension bridges. They call it a hybrid with cable stays and gravity anchored. Not only is it used for automobile traffic, but it also carries pedestrians.

When it opened in May 1883, it was called a marvel of engineering—and it's still an impressive sight. I'll bet I've been across that bridge a dozen times and I still love to look at it. And I'm not alone. Thousands of people who visit the Big Apple each year make sure that a trip to the Brooklyn Bridge is on their agenda.

Washington A. Roebling was the chief engineer on the bridge, and it was supposed to be the crowning achievement in his professional career. And I guess it was, at least to a certain extent. But there is someone who actually deserves more credit than he. You see, Roebling couldn't finish the job. Matter of fact, he barely got it started. When they were setting the caisson, the foundation for the bridge—which was seventy-eight feet underwater, by the way—Roebling got ill. Quite ill. It was decompression sickness. You see, they knew very little about it then. This horrible illness left the brilliant engineer paralyzed, partly blind, deaf, and mute. Not a good situation when you have a huge undertaking like the Brooklyn Bridge on your plate.

Roebling couldn't work, and no one else was willing to take on the awesome responsibilities of the job. Except one! One who knew almost nothing of construction or engineering. One who didn't even know higher math. One who had only a deep belief in Roebling's work. It wasn't easy, you can be sure of that. It was a job that would have challenged the top engineers of the time . . . much less a layman.

But that didn't stop someone who was committed. It required learning higher math and engineering . . . on the job. It required being a conduit between engineering and construction. It required learning some of the most difficult construction methods ever accomplished at that time. It required a lot.

Well, it's a little-known fact that if it hadn't been for the dedication of someone who was willing to take over as surrogate chief engineer, we may not have the Brooklyn Bridge today. So, we'd like to thank . . . her! Yes, her! Emily Roebling, the very smart and talented wife of Washington Roebling, was the primary reason that famous bridge stands today.

LITTLE-KNOWN FACT #12

The Man in the Fast Lane

When Terry was behind the wheel of a fast car, he felt freedom. He didn't feel it anywhere else. Not even at his day job. And that's kind of surprising, because he was very good at his regular job. He had earned the respect of a lot of people. But when it came right down to it, it was just a job. Only on the road or the race track did Terry feel completely right.

And it had been a long road to get to where he was. A product of a broken home, he moved around a lot as a boy. He got into a little trouble with the law, too, and spent some time in reform school. But as so often happens, the U.S. Marine Corps straightened him out. Well, it even took the marines a little time. He once went AWOL for two weeks. He did time in the brig for that stunt.

By all accounts he started to settle down after that, but Terry was still restless. That's when he discovered the freedom of fast cars. He even started to race on a semiprofessional basis. It caused a bit of a stir, and people who knew him from his other job began to wonder if Terry had some kind of a death wish, driving cars at dangerous speeds the way he did. He certainly didn't need the money, but he couldn't help it. He even started to design and build race cars, always looking for ways to make them better.

And to everyone's surprise, including Terry's, he turned out to be pretty good at it.

His cars, whether driven by himself for other drivers, started to win races fairly often. But you see, it wasn't just the speed or the race itself, but rather the image that Terry liked. This was the fast lane, and this was where he wanted to be. And he started to wonder about ways to enhance that sleek, fast image in his cars. He went to work, and he threw himself into his creations so completely that he turned down some very lucrative projects in his other career. But in a few months, he had it.

You see, Terry thought sports cars were all great except for one thing—the seats. He thought car seats all looked the same, a bit like the couch in your grandmother's living room. It didn't fit the image a sports car should project. So Terry came up with the idea for a new kind of seat, something perfect for a new age of automobiles, for the freedom that went with a fast car. He called it a "bucket seat."

And the auto world loved it.

Even the people at his day job had to admit that Terry had come up with something pretty special. It's a shame we don't remember Terry as the inventor of the bucket seat, because he did invent them. No, we remember him now as the star of such movies as *The Great Escape* and *The Towering Inferno*. Yep, it's a little-known fact that the bucket seat was invented by the great actor Terrence Steve McQueen.

LITTLE-KNOWN FACT #13

The Soldiers' Friend

Probably not too many of us have ever visited the historic sites in Troy, New York. But like any city that's been around since before the Revolution, it has its share of them.

Now, most people who have been there—and I have to confess right now that I haven't—say it's a pretty town, located like it is right on the Hudson River. Some of the early buildings still stand alongside the towering oaks and stately Victorian mansions. But Troy's biggest attraction lies just north of the town itself, in the Oakwood Cemetery. Here visitors can still pay their respects to the city's most famous citizen: Samuel Wilson.

You would have to call Samuel an ordinary man, really. But like most early Americans, he lived in extraordinary times. Samuel was just nine years old when Paul Revere came racing past the Wilson family home right outside Boston on his wild midnight ride to Lexington. Two of Samuel's older brothers (and he had eight of them) fought with General Washington in the Revolutionary War. Samuel was one of thirteen children born to one of three brothers who had immigrated from Scotland. His family eventually ended up in New Hampshire and, at twenty-four, Samuel came west with his brother Ebenezer to seek his fortune. Well, west in those days was still pretty much east, and he found himself settling down in Troy, New York.

Now, two enterprising young men like these couldn't help but make good. In just a few years, the brothers opened their own meatpacking business . . . and did pretty well at it, too. In 1805, they advertised that they could butcher out 150 cows a day—quite a feat even now. The pair built a dock down on the river and started shipping off salted pork and beef in huge barrels made of white oak.

By the time the new nation found itself again at odds with England in the War of 1812, business was booming in Troy and for Samuel and Ebenezer. Troy was a bustling town, prosperous and bent on enjoying everything good this young country had to offer. Right outside town, the American army built barracks that would house six thousand of the northern troops while they rested between battles. And the military couldn't have picked a better place.

Troy boasted its fair share of taverns and meeting-houses. And Samuel was a frequent visitor at both. People who knew him described him as "jolly, genial, and generous." He made friends as easy as breathing . . . and was a sight to see, too. He was a tall gentleman who wore his gray hair rather long and dressed in the height of fashion. When those six thousand troops needed meat, they naturally went to Samuel and Ebenezer. And the brothers dutifully began butchering and packing their order for five thousand barrels of prime meat.

Now, to understand how Samuel won his fame, you have to first understand the times. America was still young, mighty young, and the federal government was still fairly weak. Populations were strung out in colonies all along the East Coast with an untamed, frightening wilderness bordering the entire western side.

What soldiers needed in this war was a sense of unity. And they took it where they could find it—in this case, from the abbreviation *U.S.* they found stamped on the sides of their barrels of meat. Now, today we know that *U.S.* stands for "United States," but back then, that acronym was rarely used. And few people had ever heard of it. But the men stationed in Troy did know Samuel. They drank with him in the taverns, hailed him on the streets. With thirteen brothers and sisters, Samuel had a whole slew of nephews and nieces, many of them running around town calling him uncle. And after a while, so did everybody else. So the soldiers of the War of 1812 took one look at that *U.S.* symbol and thought of Samuel: the friend who kept them fed. It's a little-known fact that those early soldiers took to calling themselves "Uncle Sam's boys." And so a national icon was born. The man you see pointing at you from time to time on military posters, well, he was a real person. The inspiration for our own beloved Uncle Sam was Samuel Wilson, a butcher from Troy.

LITTLE-KNOWN FACT #14

War Games

It came as a surprise. The captain on duty had pretty much thought that things would escalate into some real fighting—just not this quickly. Tensions between the North and the South had been getting worse for years now. On the surface, the country was wrestling with the question of slavery. But if you know your history, then you also know that slavery was really just the most visible sign of the deep divisions within our country. So extensive was the mistrust between North and South that every effort at compromise seemed merely to delay the inevitable.

And now this young captain was at the forefront. He was sitting on top of the wall at Fort Sumter in Charleston Bay, South Carolina, surrounded by Confederate forces. He was a captain for the Union army all right. After all, he vehemently opposed slavery and thought the talk of secession was traitorous. He was a New Yorker . . . a graduate of West Point . . . now an army captain, and being stationed at Fort Sumter was like being in the camp of the enemy. He wrote that to his wife, and told her that he believed this war was inescapable.

President Abraham Lincoln had asked to see those letters to learn firsthand what life was like for Union troops in the South. This captain was no beginner, though . . . no, he had fought in wars before, against Mexico and the Seminole nation. And he had led the fighting on the Texas frontier. He knew what war was like, and he knew this one would be different. This time it wasn't some other country or some foreign enemy. No, this time it would be brother against brother, neighbor against neighbor, father against son.

Suddenly it started. The first shots from the Confederate troops bombarded Fort Sumter with cannon fire. The incensed captain immediately knew what he had to do— he ordered his men to return fire and lit the first cannon fuse himself. The battle raged for hours . . . and the next day the United States declared war on the Confederacy.

What happened to that captain who fired that very first shot for the Union, you might ask? You would think that we would all remember him for that first shot . . . but we don't! Oh, we remember him all right, but not for fighting the courageous fight. No, we remember him for something far more entertaining . . . something that is still very popular today . . . especially in the summer. You see, it's a little-known fact that the Union captain who fired the first shot by the North in the Civil War was none other than Abner Doubleday, the legendary inventor of the game of baseball.

LITTLE-KNOWN FACT #15

The Two-Time Loser

In the year 1836, certain liberty-loving Texans declared their independence from Mexico and unfurled their Lone Star flag. From that time forward the war was on. Mexican forces swept ferociously into Texas territory. There was a certain fellow from central Mexico who fought with the Mexican army. He was a descendant of the mighty Aztecs, much experienced in battle. In San Antonio, at the Alamo, a brave band of nearly two hundred American men were trapped by the Mexican army. They were wiped out to a man—men like Davy Crockett and Jim Bowie.

Of course, we've all heard about the cry that went up: "Remember the Alamo."

About a month later that same Mexican army ran into Sam Houston and the American army. The mighty Mexican army was soundly defeated and sent back to Mexico, and that little Mexican fellow along with them. But the defeat that his country had suffered didn't sit very well with him. He decided to go where the opportunities were. To him that brash new country to the north seemed the place to go. So he booked passage and moved to Staten Island in New York City. One of the possessions he took with him was something he had enjoyed from his childhood in southern Mexico—the sap from a tree native to his home called the chicola tree. This gummy resin chould be chewed for hours without losing its consistency. The fellow knew he wouldn't be able to obtain it in New York, so he took a whole barrel of it along with him.

Now, people have always loved to chew—practically anything: beeswax, tobacco, paraffin, tar, you name it. And Americans were no different. Always looking for something else to try every chance they got. As the little Mexican fellow took an occasional chew of his prized resin, many of his New York friends also tried it. And they loved it.

One of his acquaintances, a pharmacist, started experimenting by adding different syrups and flavors to the resin, like cherry and peppermint. That gummy resin now had a purpose in life: "chewing gum"! That's how it got invented. And that pharmacist gave it a name, taken from the chicola tree. He coined the term *chicklets*. A little later Mr. Wrigley came along and added a few twists of his own, and he brought the product to nationwide popularity.

But about that little Mexican fellow who was responsible for all this . . . he went back to Mexico, and there in 1876 died in poverty. He was one of those men whom fate touches in a remarkable way. For you see, to his dying day he remembered two great failures.

For one: He had failed to cash in on the multibillion-dollar chewing gum revolution he'd started. But even before that, back when he was with the army, he had suffered a humiliating defeat at the hands of the American army. And it was his fault. For you see, his name was General Antonio López de Santa Anna. Think about it the next time you unwrap a stick of chewing gum.

LITTLE-KNOWN FACT #16

The Secret Underground City

In the Chinese language, the word for China means "center" or "middle." Throughout history, the Chinese people have always considered their country, their culture, to be the center of the earth. And that, folks, is just one of the reasons that so many things about China remained a mystery, a secret, for thousands of years. And although visitors from the outside world are now traveling into China every day, many things from the past still remain—well, a mystery.

Today, anthropologists and archaeologists are finding clues to the past and the long-silent places of ancient times are ready to reveal their most amazing secrets.

In 1969, a network of secret tunnels was discovered that showed, once again, how these proud people preferred to stay together, and to keep their activities a secret. The Westerner who first cast a light into these long-forgotten tunnels must have been amazed. On the walls of the hidden passageways was Chinese writing that told of the illegal gambling parlors that once resounded with the excited activity of the men and women who came here to take a chance on fortune. Down a dusty corridor were cooking stoves where clandestine meals were prepared for the select few who knew of the existence of these secret kitchens and the exotic fare that was served. What meals would have been prepared here that were not acceptable aboveground? That were never shared with the people walking overhead?

And why were there laundry rooms hidden away in these secret tunnels? Surely, any of this could have been done up above, in the harsh daylight of the busy city just a few feet over their heads? Or was there reason to hide all this?

Imagine exploring these dark chambers and coming upon a real operating subterranean Buddhist temple—with solid-gold wallpaper? Well, the answers to these questions may never be known. And even the reason why these secret Chinese tunnels were dug in the first place may always be a riddle . . . especially to the Sooners above. Sooners? Yep it's a little-known fact that these secret Chinese tunnels existed—and were recently discovered—about twenty feet down, right in the middle of Oklahoma City, USA!

LITTLE-KNOWN FACT #17

Warfare Meets the Twentieth Century?

Seems like all kids love secret codes. Can you remember the thrill of sending a secret message to your best buddy back in school—making plans for the sunny afternoon you could see out there beyond your dusty schoolbooks, or confessing to a secret crush on some heartthrob across the classroom? I'll bet you can remember how nervous you felt, passing notes while the teacher lectured on. When I was a kid, they'd make you stand up and read what you'd written to the whole class. Probably still do. Makes you wonder whether some of those famous spies and codemakers got their start the same place you probably did—thinking of some way to let your buddy on the other side of the room know who you hoped would be your date for the spring dance.

Maybe it was some mischievous note-passing kid who grew up to be the one America's military leaders turned to back in 1914, when they were faced with their greatest codemaking challenge to date. It was the eve of World War I—the Great War—the war to end all wars, it was called. Trouble was brewing in Europe, and American military leaders knew that it wouldn't be long before their troops were sent overseas. They were also aware that new technology had created a new and modern style of wartime communications: the telegraph. That one invention made it possible to transmit vital information across long distances. Generals who had once commanded troops from a nearby hilltop—using things like pigeons and torches and couriers—could now coordinate the movements of troops hundreds of miles away. As they prepared to enter into the greatest fray in military history, America's leaders knew that they were dealing with a new kind of army—and a new kind of war.

Our generals had no intention of getting by without the telegraph. But they'd never be able to use the crucial new communication tool unless their codemakers could come up with a decoding device that could be distributed to operators in the field. It had to allow users to change the code keys continually—in case an enemy spy, listening in, managed to crack the code.

With the Great War closing in, American codemakers worked feverishly to create a portable device that could generate a constantly changing code. They knew that unless they could come up with something, American troops were at risk as never before.

The solution came in the nick of time. As American troop ships pulled from the docks, the codemakers came up with the M-94—a system of revolving disks that allowed radio operators to create a brand-new code each time they transmitted across enemy lines. It was a breakthrough in communications technology that became the army standard and served as a codemaking protoype for the modern age.

They say the Great War was the first truly modern war; that the changes the military made back then would alter the face of battle forever. The troops returning home in 1918 would become part of a modern world that continued to depend on the very latest in technology.

It might have surprised the codemakers who brought the army into that modern age to learn that the M-94 was the direct result of another discovery a year or two before. Far from the heat of battle, in a dusty library in Virginia, a scholar organizing some old paperwork stumbled across a set of notes made by a local landowner . . . a man who had come up with an idea he called a cipher wheel, somewhere around 1790.

It wasn't surprising no one had heard of it before. After all, the inventor hadn't taken the trouble to patent it, although he did happen to be the head of the U.S. patent office at the time. It's a little-known fact that the protoype for the M-94 was actually invented a hundred years before modern technology would make it a necessity—the brainchild of a hopeless tinkerer named Thomas Jefferson.

LITTLE-KNOWN FACT #18

The Young Mystic

The year was 1930, and in his New York laboratory, Nobel Prize recipient Dr. Alexis Carrel prepared to operate. As tradition demanded, he slipped into his long black robe and pulled over his head the heavy hood that covered his face completely, save for narrow slits for his eyes. He opened the door into darkness. Inside the black-walled operating room, his assistants—also robed and hooded completely in black—glided silently about. Brief glimpses of their eyes gave reassurance of the human forms beneath. An occasional whisper broke the silence as Alexis carefully laid his instruments out, ready for use.

The animal Dr. Carrel had chosen for the experiment lay anesthetized on the operating table, spotlighted by the single shaft of light that sliced through the darkness from the narrow skylight above. Carrel knew his latest surgery would provide him with valuable research material, as it had done so often in the past. As the doctor prepared to begin the operation, the door opened . . . and a second black-robed figure moved silently toward the table. The newcomer, Charles, would be forever transformed by his experience at the side of Alexis Carrel, who was to become his mentor and partner in mystical inquiry for the remainder of the older man's life—and perhaps beyond.

The two were, physically, a study in contrasts. Carrel was a short, stout Frenchman. His American colleague Charles was tall and lean. Carrel had made his reputation in the world of medicine, and had spent eighteen years in continuous experimentation into the nature of life and death. Charles had been drawn to Carrel's reputation as a mystic as well as a physician. The younger man had won world acclaim for his extraordinary mechanical abilities. But his true passion was inquiry into the supernatural—especially the same questions of life after death that preoccupied the older physician. Charles had spent years—and would spend the rest of his life—inquiring into the same philosophical questions that had inspired Carrel in a lifetime of very unconventional research.

Charles had experienced many brushes with death, beginning during his childhood on a Minnesota farm. This constant contact with the fragility of life . . . combined with his vivid, recurring dreams of a world beyond normal human experience . . . had led him around the world in search of mystics who could answer his many questions about the nature of life and death. He felt that a destiny beyond the understanding of either man had drawn him to join with Alexis Carrel that day in 1930.

Together, the men spent the next five years working continuously and feverishly to develop a means to cheat death—a way that organs removed from a dying body could be kept alive for transplantation or repair. Though the practical applications were obvious, both men felt that their work had metaphysical meaning and implications beyond their humanitarian aims. The idea of an organ suspended in eternal life fascinated each of them.

Their efforts were more successful than they had dared hope. The "Perfusion pump" perfected some years later turned out to be capable of keeping organs alive for long periods of time, separate from the host body. It was suddently possible for surgeons to repair—and eventually to replace—damaged organs, saving the lives of thousands.

As amazing as this achievement was, Charles was to go on to great glory in another feat . . . one that captured the world's attention and changed the course of history. It's a little-known fact that the young mystic beneath the black robe that day in 1930 . . . the man who developed the first successful artificial heart to preserve human tissue . . . was none other than the all-American hero of aviation: Charles Lindbergh.

LITTLE-KNOWN FACT #19

The Jack-of-All-Trades

Most of us don't expect our youngsters to bring home a paycheck, but when young Eric's family left Hungary and settled in New York in the 1880s, he had to. And Eric's choice of occupation—well, it was just what you might expect from an eight-year-old boy. He got a job traveling with a circus and performing on the high trapeze. But Eric wasn't really all that good on the high swings. Just a year later he quit the Big Top and settled down at a new job: making ties in a garment sweatshop. Still, Eric had been bitten—yes, bitten by the show-business bug. It was in his blood now. And he vowed he'd be back.

As far as anyone can tell, there were only two things Eric was really good at. One of those was running. It's said that he could outrun just about anything. But even so, he couldn't run as well as he could swim. Why, he even taught himself to hold his breath underwater for four minutes. And that's quite a feat even today.

If you ask me, I'd say those were probably two pretty thin talents when it came to building a career in show business. After all, Eric couldn't sing or dance or tell jokes. But that didn't bother him much. Believe it or not, he took those humble athletic skills and made a name for himself in vaudeville.

One thing Eric counted on in his act was people's love of a good mystery. With a little sleight of hand and some dark lights, Eric gave his audiences a good dose of the mysterious. But the truth was, Eric didn't really like mysteries. No, he was one of those guys who thought that if you looked hard enough, you could find an explanation for just about everything. Why, if he hadn't been in show business, I bet Eric would have made a good scientist, and it's not just his sleight of hand that makes me think so.

You see, he was something of a pioneer aviator. In 1910, he became the first person on record to fly a plane in Australia. And when it came to the deep, dark seas, Eric did his part there, too. It was pretty common for ocean explorers to drown simply because they ran out of air and got trapped deep underwater in one of those bulky, dangerous diving suits they used back then. Well, it's a little-known fact that Eric holds a patent for a special kind of diving suit . . . the kind that a diver could break out of quickly and escape back to the water's surface if he got into trouble. In 1921, Eric registered this new escapable diving suit.

And you could say that this was one inventor who knew what he was doing. You see, Eric used another name when he was up on stage: Harry Houdini.

LITTLE-KNOWN FACT #20

The Great Dog Fennel Experiment

Chappy had seen the future: dog fennel. He knew that a number of Indian tribes had used it to make a tea or drink. Some people call it mayweed; it's used to treat illnesses. He believed that natural, herbal medicines were the key to good health. And he certainly wasn't the only one—after all, a lot of folks think that if a good natural cure exists, it sure beats a trip to the doctor.

Mayweed was considered a top cure for colds and fevers, and Chappy felt that if he could spread the word about dog fennel, he'd be doing the world a heap of good. He saw, though, that knowing about and believing in dog fennel wasn't enough—people had to be able to get their hands on the plant.

So he started traveling through Ohio and Indiana, passing out dog fennel seeds. When farmers seemed reluctant to plant these seeds, he'd go ahead and do it himself, sometimes when the farmers weren't looking. He was happy, knowing they'd thank him later. But let me tell you why the plant is called dog fennel: because it smells something like a wet dog!

Real fennel is a beautiful, sweet-smelling aromatic plant that's delicious when used in salads, or sautéed and served by itself. Some cooks put fennel in stews, and fennel seeds are used in many Mediterranean cuisines. Dog fennel, though . . . well, let's just say that not even dogs will eat the stuff. But that didn't stop Chappy. He was determined to spread the mayweed gospel and get people healthy. But soon people who had tried treating headaches with dog fennel discovered that not only did it smell terrible, it didn't work. What's more, it proved to be something akin to Attila the Hun in its ability to take over cultivated soil—that stuff grows like . . . well, like a weed! And farmers had to spend weeks getting rid of their unwanted dog fennel fields.

So all Chappy really accomplished was antagonizing darn near everybody who came in contact with the plant. Yes! The great dog fennel experiment was a complete bust. But don't worry about Chappy. He went on to find a crop that people liked a lot and actually *wanted* to grow.

It's a little-known fact that John Chapman was practically run out of every town in the Midwest. Before he changed his game plan and gained fame planting . . . apple trees. John Chapman. But you know him as the real Johnny Appleseed.

LITTLE-KNOWN FACT #21

The Doorman

If you'd been lucky enough to visit the old Ed Butler Standard Theater in St. Louis back around 1900 or so, odds are you would've had yourself a pretty good time. The way folks tell it, they had a little bit of everything. Some early jazz and ragtime music. A ventriloquist or two. And if you needed a good laugh, slapstick comedy and vaudeville acts were there, too.

And you could always count on the dancers. Any way you looked at it, the Standard Theater was the place to be.

Now, if you were really on the ball, you might have even taken notice of old Alex, who worked there as the doorman. Of course, he wasn't much to look at, really. And if you bothered to make his acquaintance, more than likely you'd have thought life had been kind of hard on him. What was left of his hair—and there wasn't much—was solid white.

Those who knew him were struck by the deep ridges that lined his face. His back was a little stooped, and every time it rained, he would complain to the patrons that his rheumatism was acting up. If you stopped to talk a minute, Alex wouldn't have had a whole lot to say. He'd just nod and smile and open the door for you. Few people cared enough to ask him about his past, and those who did found out it was not a subject he was willing to talk about. If he answered you at all, it would be short and terse—a response that let you know the subject was closed.

And for good reason, I might add.

The last couple of decades in Alex's life might not have been too exciting. A doorman's job is pretty docile, and he never talked much about the good old days when he still had a full head of hair and a slim figure. Or about the crowd he ran with in his youth. But if he had told folks about the old days, they would have gotten an earful, that's for sure.

The truth is, folks, you never know who you're talking to when you meet someone new. Because it's a little-known fact that Alex the doorman had lived most of his younger years as an outlaw with a huge price on his head. There was a time when every lawman in the country was after him and his brother . . . Jesse.

Yes, that quiet doorman was in fact none other than Alexander Frank James.

LITTLE-KNOWN FACT #22

Tragedy on the Seas?

Now you might have already heard enough to last you a lifetime . . . but to some of us, it's a story that bears repeating. And really, it's not all that hard to understand why. The tragic history of the *Titanic* has fascinated a good many of us for nearly a century. The ship was the stuff that dreams are made of; a slice of the elegant life. And even the tragedy itself, well, it wasn't your usual run-of-the-mill horror picture. Just think how hard it is to forget—and I'm sure you've imagined it—the women and children slowly drifting away in lifeboats, while the fathers and husbands and crew of the *Titanic* stand on the decks. Just waiting to sink into the icy water. And all because there were too few lifeboats.

That's the really sad part. Historians tell us that not one single person was injured from the crash with the iceberg itself. But because there weren't enough lifeboats to keep everybody afloat until they could be rescued, fifteen hundred crew and passengers went down with the ship.

The disaster spawned a mighty loud call for reform in marine safety, even though voyages across the Atlantic were fairly safe. Of the six million people who'd crossed in the ten years right before the *Titanic*'s first voyage, only nine had drowned. But one tragedy of this magnitude was enough. A "lifeboats for all" movement swept across America and Europe.

But there was disagreement even then. Boats often sank quickly. And the idea that everyone would have time to jump into a lifeboat was ridiculous to some. Besides that, lifeboats were notoriously heavy, weighing more than a ton apiece and adding to the top heaviness of a boat. But in March 1915, the U.S. Congress passed a law that called for ships to carry lifeboats for at least 75 percent of passengers, while rafts would have to do for the others. Even so, experts in marine travel raised grave doubts about all of these lifeboats. On July 24, 1915, an American trade magazine called the *Marine Journal* ran an editorial that called this law "ludicrous." In seventy-five years of oceangoing travel, no disaster parallel to the *Titanic* had ever occurred, they claimed, and it wouldn't be possible to cause a similar accident even if it was tried on purpose.

But on that very same day, something occurred that both proved their idea that more lifeboats didn't necessarily mean saved lives and disproved their claim that the *Titanic* was a once-in-a-lifetime freak accident.

In the early-morning hours, a steamer called the *Eastland* was being boarded by twenty-five hundred Western Electric employees ready for a day of fun and adventure. The vessel had just received clearance to take almost five hundred additional passengers on board and so had decked out its top with the extra lifeboats that would accommodate them. With the weight of these extra lifeboats, and the extra passengers all standing on the side of the ship facing the water, the steamer started listing, or leaning. At first, at just a twenty-five-degree angle, it was great fun for the passengers—just part of the festivities. But slowly, yet surely, the ship kept leaning . . . a bit more . . . and more!

And more, until finally it gently settled on its port side and, soon after, turned completely over. The consequences were disastrous. More than eight hundred passengers drowned. It was one of the worst maritime disasters in

American history, the sixth worst according to lives lost. More actual passengers perished in this accident than did on the *Titanic*. But it's a little-known fact that this disaster was a different kind of marine tragedy. Rather than passengers drowning way out on the high seas, the Eastland was still partially tied to the docks of the Chicago River. And the eight hundred people who drowned were just a few short feet away from the bustling shores of downtown Chicago.

LITTLE-KNOWN FACT #23

The Power Behind the Throne

Edith was a widow at forty-three. She really hadn't given any thought to getting married again. Her late husband had been a wealthy jeweler and left her financially secure. Her days were spent in the company of good friends and a number of social functions. She had decided she didn't need another man in her life. But you know how fate is . . . the minute you think you know what you want, something comes along to change your mind.

That's pretty much what happened when Edith accepted an invitation to tea from a friend. The tea was being held at the home of her friend's cousin, who was a well-known and powerful man. As Edith and her friend were enjoying the socializing, the gentleman of the house arrived. Wouldn't you know it, Edith was almost instantly smitten with him. And why not: He was well spoken, mannerly, cultured. He was fifteen years older than Edith, and he was a widower himself.

Well, one thing led to another, as things do, and Edith married Woody a few months later. She was absolutely devoted to him, and he to her. They traveled everywhere together, and he consulted her on all decisions, whether large or small. One of Woody's friends grumbled that it was impossible to talk to him anymore, because every time he tried, he was always busy whispering to Edith. It wasn't long before Edith wielded a little influence of her own, and she used it to support her husband's many projects.

By all accounts, they were one of the happiest, most successful couples in America. But then Woody became very ill. Many said that he would never be the same. Some of his closest associates suggested that he should step down from his position. Woody seemed to agree. Edith, on the other hand, would hear none of it. And when these same "gentlemen" asked who was going to do his job, she said she'd simply do it herself! And she did. She set it up so that the only people who got in to see Woody were herself and his doctor. She threw herself into his job. She signed off on all major projects, and got new ones started.

When some of the underlings grumbled about the way things were being run, she fired them and replaced them with people she knew were loyal to her husband. She was tough in negotiations with his rivals, and she never gave an inch. Edith made it clear that she spoke for her husband, and if someone didn't like it, she showed them the door. By all accounts, she ran things! And it appears she ran them as well as her husband did, maybe even better. Through all this, she protected her husband and his condition. She didn't allow any public announcements about his illness.

As far as the rest of world was concerned, everything

was normal. Never mind that he wasn't seen in public for nearly three years!

Well, finally the time came for Edith and her husband to retire, and she took care of him until the day he died. She was a remarkable woman, more so than you might suspect.

You see, it's a little-known fact that although we have never elected a woman president, we did have one. And a good one. Edith Wilson served in her husband's absence, almost completely running the country after her husband, Woodrow Wilson, suffered a stroke.

LITTLE-KNOWN FACT #24

The Dramatic Death of Chief Sitting Bull

Accounts vary about how it started. But how it ended is clear. One side said that the soliders didn't have to treat him so rough. The other side said that he was uncooperative and was resisting arrest. As with most things, the truth probably lies somewhere in the middle, but regardless of how it started, when it was over . . . Chief Sitting Bull, famed leader of the Sioux nation, was dead.

Most of us remember the name Sitting Bull as belonging to the great and powerful medicine man who was the spiritual leader of the Sioux at the battle of Little Big Horn. But many don't know that years later, famed frontiersman and showman Buffalo Bill Cody took the great Sitting Bull and his favorite horse on a worldwide tour in his Wild West show. When the rigors of travel got too hard on the aging medicine man . . . he came home.

For ten years he'd been living under a grant of amnesty from the U. S. government. But now another Sioux leader was telling members of the Sioux nation that they could defeat the United States, and word reached the authorities that Sitting Bull was helping to create a rebellion. Forty-three Native American soldiers from the U. S. Army arrived to arrest Sitting Bull.

When the arresting Indian officers seemed to treat the elderly chief roughly, Sitting Bull's followers became enraged. Suddenly a shot rang out and Sitting Bull slumped over. The air was filled with tension; people hadn't expected this to happen. Then for no apparent reason, Sitting Bull's horse leapt into the air and began to cavort wildly. He jumped from side to side and reared up and swung back and forth. Then he lay on the ground and kicked his legs. Sitting Bull's followers were convinced that their chief had sent his spirit into the horse, and they saw it as an order to get revenge for their murdered leader. Fierce fighting erupted. As the shooting continued, the horse continued to leap into the air, prance on his hind legs, and roll on the ground. Inspired by the horse's actions, the outnumbered Sioux fought on. When the shooting finally stopped, fourteen people lay dead, including the legendary Sitting Bull.

Did Sitting Bull send his spirit into that horse?

The Native Americans who were there say he did . . . but, we know one more thing. It's a little-known fact that Sitting Bull's horse was a trained and seasoned professional in Buffalo Bill's traveling Wild West show. Each time the horse heard a gunshot, it was his cue to begin performing his Wild West dance routine.

LITTLE-KNOWN FACT #25

The Designing Woman

Funny as it may seem, we don't know her first name—
only that she was the daughter of a shopkeeper named
Rufas Skeel. But we do know that she had an eye for
beauty. And she was quite an artist. She loved to paint still
lifes, and that took up most of her spare time.

Miss Skeel didn't sit around painting all day, though.
She had to attend to her chores of sewing and needlework,
as was expected of all young ladies in the 1800s. But one
day, while browsing around in her father's store, she found
some really fine muslin fabric from a textile mill owned by
Benjamin and Robert Knight. She loved the new fabric. The
soft texture felt good on her skin, and it was easy to cut and
sew. But the customers seemed to be ignoring it.

Well, she knew that if the customers just tried it, they
would like this wonderful muslin, but she didn't quite
know how to make the plain white cloth seem more at-
tractive. She worried it around in her head for a while and
finally came up with a grand idea. Miss Skeel went to
work with her paints and paper and made several paintings of a swar apple, a family favorite at the Skeel house.
When the paintings of the rosy apples were dry, she
pasted them to the muslin material—and sure enough, the
cloth with the paintings attached was the first to sell.

In fact, the paintings were so popular that soon she was
painting grapes, pears, and cherries to paste onto the
Knight mill material, too. Now you have to understand
that this was quite a departure from the normal. Fabric up

to that point was kind of like a Model T: you could have any color you want, as long as it was black. Well, not all fabric was black, of course, but designs on fabric was nearly unheard of. A few pin stripes here and there, and that was about it!

So when this young woman started decorating fabric, people really took notice.

As you might guess, Robert Knight, the owner of the textile mill, took notice pretty quick that one store was selling more of his new cloth than nearly all the others combined. Fact was, the little country store was selling quite a few mill materials. Robert Knight decided to investigate personally, and found that Miss Skeel's artwork was making the difference—and that gave him an idea. He talked it over with his brother and soon the young woman's pictures were copied and printed and appeared as labels on all the cloth that came from the Knight mill. That was in 1871.

Before long, the labels showed a combination of an apple, some grapes, and some gooseberries—and they still do today. Yep, it's a little-known fact that one young lady's love of painting and wonderful imagination led to the first label ever used on a bolt of cloth and to what we know today as Fruit of the Loom.

LITTLE-KNOWN FACT #26

The Great Fire

Used to be, fires were a whole lot more terrible than they are now. I'm not saying that they're still not a great tragedy . . . because they certainly are, especially when the house that's gone was yours, or when someone you loved didn't make it through. It's just been in the last few years, after all, that we've started to see a turn for the better.

A few decades ago, somewhere around twelve thousand Americans lost their lives in fires every year, and that's a staggering figure. Today we can thank modern fire science . . . because that number's fallen to less than five thousand a year. In 1980, three million fires blazed across America; fifteen years later, that number was down to less than two million. But don't feel too good about all this improvement. The truth is, the United States still has one of the highest fire rates of any Western country . . . and hardly a day goes by that people don't die in fires.

If you take a good look at history, you'll notice that America's always had a problem with fires—since the very beginning. But you've got to remember that the United States was what you might call a "boom" country. Entire towns would shoot up overnight. And they could be built pretty quickly and cheaply with wood . . . and wood burns. Now add that to the understanding that fires used to be fought in this country with buckets of water, and it's a wonder any town survived at all.

Most of us find it hard to imagine an entire town burning down, but it happened all the time back a hundred years ago. From 1860 to 1880, the survival of the whole state of Nevada was a near thing. Reno, Carson City, Virginia City were all virtually wiped out in infernos.

In the later years of the nineteenth century and early into the twentieth, horrific fires blazed through Boston, Baltimore, New York City, and San Francisco . . . scorching through the major areas of business and leaving thousands homeless. And then there was that great fire that raged through a city in the North.

It happened on a dry, windy day, from all accounts, following a long, hot summer. Just the right setting for a fire disaster of epic proportions. Afterward, an entire town lay in ruins. Some reports put the number of dead at about twelve hundred, others at fifteen hundred, but nobody could be 100 percent sure. There simply wasn't enough left after that fire to tell. The heat was so intense it split boulders in two. The firefighters threw down their buckets and ran for their lives ... and nobody blamed them. This was the kind of fire that a man and a bucket just didn't stand a chance against. Witnesses said the very air was burning.

By now you're probably pretty sure I'm talking about Chicago, where that one old cow supposedly burned down most of the town on the night of October 8, 1871 ... but you're wrong. You've got to travel three hundred miles north of Chicago to the state of Wisconsin and a boomtown called Peshtigo to locate the remnants of the fire that's been called the worst in American history ... where a single fire ravished twenty-four hundred square miles of forest and homesteads and killed a thousand more Americans than did the one in Chicago.

It's a little-known fact that, odd as it seems, that fire occurred on the very night, at the very instant that Chicago was also burning down. But by the time the few, suffering survivors of Peshtigo could get word to the outside world, Chicago had already grabbed the headlines ... and the memories of the rest of the world.

LITTLE-KNOWN FACT #27

The Devil's Day?

John Pickering couldn't believe what he was hearing. He knew this matter was going to come up for debate sooner or later. It had to; it had its origins in the old country, and everything that came over from the old country was suspect sooner or later.

But this was just a holiday . . . a tradition!

As John stood there in the church speaking his mind and telling the leaders of the Massachusetts Bay colony that he just couldn't see how outlawing such a simple celebration would make any real difference, he was shouted down by the leaders. There was Hollis Mann, the leader of the opposing group, raising his voice and getting very excited. This celebration and acknowledgment of such a sacrilegious day could not be allowed to stand. Especially here in the midst of the New World. Here, where the Pilgrims had settled to escape the persecution and traditions of the Old World, back across the ocean.

And even their preacher, William Lloyd, spoke against it. It had its traditions in hedonism and devil worship, he said. It smacks of the druids and the ancient black magic beliefs of the builders of Stonehenge. It is a direct throwback to the Dark Ages, Lloyd said. And it appeared that the congregation was going along with its spiritual leaders.

But John just didn't think it was right. After all, even if it did have some basis in pagan rituals, that certainly wasn't the case any longer. And what was celebrated now was some simple things. Some dressed up in costumes and even gave food, and small gifts to others. It seemed to be a time of good-natured fun, and John just didn't see how it was going to hurt the colony to continue the holiday tradition. But he was certainly running up against serious opposition.

Finally, Hollis Mann spoke again, and told John that if John didn't see it their way—well, he might be a witch! John sat down and didn't say another word. They took a vote that day, in 1659, and outlawed that pagan holiday, making it against the law to celebrate with the wearing of costumes, or resting from labor, or feasting of any kind. It's a little-known fact that law lasted almost twenty years . . . until the residents of the Massachusetts Bay colony could once again celebrate Christmas!

LITTLE-KNOWN FACT #28

The One That Got Away

Sam had to admit that this fellow was certainly sold on his new gizmo. For the last hour he had regaled Sam with visions of how his new invention was going to change the world. But Sam was leery!

He'd heard this "going to change the world" story before, from other people. It seemed that it was just one fantastic invention or business deal after another. Problem was, none of these deals ever seemed to work out, at least for Sam. But he knew he had to do something if he was going to continue to live in the style in which he was accustomed. He was getting older, and he wouldn't mind slowing down a bit and taking it a little easier, and he figured that he ought to have some investments working for him so he could do just that.

And in the late 1800s and early 1900s that wasn't really all that easy. You see, Social Security hadn't come along yet, much less things like individual retirement accounts or 401Ks or money market accounts. No, back then, if you weren't lucky enough or smart enough to save up or invest your money for your retirement . . . you just had to work until you died. Or depend on kinfolk to take care of you. And Sam had kind of become known by inventors as someone who would put up seed money on a new project.

Now, Sam had been pretty successful in his life. He was a popular writer. His works were known nearly all over the world. He made a lot of money. He traveled constantly and he rather enjoyed living the good life, so he spent money rather freely, too. He often wrote about his travels, from his days as a boy on the Mississippi River to dining with the royalty of Europe and the teeming dens of the Orient. He didn't always use his own name to write; often he wrote under the name Mark Twain. But regardless of which name Sam Clemens used to pen his adventures and stories, he was well known and loved. And he was also smart enough to know that if he didn't start investing his money, he might not have any for his old age.

Over the years, he had tried many investments in an effort to secure some retirement income. There was that shoe deal, where a fella convinced him that one style shoe would be a big seller for poor and rich alike. Then there was the time he invested in the riverboat deal—kind of a throwback to his childhood, I guess. But those investments and many others . . . well, they just all seemed to go south on him. Then there was this fella with yet one more deal. Sam had to admit that this one sounded good, and the fella really didn't want that much money—only five hundred dollars to buy into the deal. But Sam Clemens had lost so much money from bad investment schemes that he just couldn't see his way clear to put any more of his hard-earned cash out on another get-rich-quick deal. So, after struggling with his conscience for a while, Sam decided that he would get out of the business of investing.

Well, it's a little-known fact that Sam Clemens, or Mark Twain, if you wish, finally turned down someone for seed money on a new venture. And that day Mr. Thomas Alva Edison went away with only his new lightbulb in his hand.

LITTLE-KNOWN FACT #29

Jumpin' Jehosophat!

You know, folks, there's an old saying: Don't judge a book by its cover. I don't think that was ever more true than with George. George was a very dapper man. He was well known by his friends as a handsome dresser. His suits were always custom-made by some of the finest tailors in Hollywood. He was a wine connoisseur. And by that I don't mean that he liked good wine. Oh, he did all right, but more, he knew vintages, mixes, and combinations of wines. As a matter of fact, George spent quite a goodly amount of time in France and Germany researching fine wines and becoming one of the acknowledged wine connoisseurs of our day. A quiet, unassuming man, he was often described as a man of gentile manners and gorgeous silver hair, always neatly trimmed and combed. But mostly, George was a gourmet. And I do mean *gourmet*.

He was a fabulous chef. And he was more than willing to share many of his fine recipes with his friends and fans. As the story goes, one day while shopping at the famed lakeside market in Hollywood, where most people did their shopping for fresh produce and other groceries, George noticed the little snack bar/deli was closed. This was a popular little eatery in the area. When he inquired why it was closed, he was told that the proprietor was ill. The people at the market were worried, since the deli was the only source of income for the owner.

George shucked his tailored coat on the spot and started cooking. Others joined in to help wait tables. The customers who gathered were in awe of the fabulous array of fine gourmet meals that started coming out of the kitchen. Word spread like wildfire that a very talented chef was cooking at the lakeside deli. For weeks people gathered every day to taste the new cooking sensation. Newspaper critics raved about the food, and the lines were backed up to the street every day. Not only had George saved the little deli for the owner, but he had created a real stir in the gourmet cooking world. The deli owner recovered and came back to work.

And it's was a good thing for George, because he had his other job to get back to. The one in which the rest of us knew him.

Don't even try to guess. But it's true: It's a little-known fact that the man who was a gourmet sensation and true wine connoisseur had to get back to his movie roles . . . with the likes of John Wayne, Roy Rogers, Gene Autry, and HopaLong Cassidy. You know him, but I'll bet you never

thought that when he was off camera, who he became was
. . . the real George: Gabby Hayes!

LITTLE-KNOWN FACT #30

Mama's Boy

Harry Burn scrambled through an office window in the
Tennessee State Capitol and crept along a third-floor ledge
to escape the angry mob that chased him. He inched his
way along that ledge and managed to get into the attic,
where he hid until his pursuers gave up the hunt. The mob
chasing Harry were all wearing red roses on their jacket
lapels. And just a few minutes earlier all had been his
friends and allies. What could cause such a change, you
ask?

Well, it was August and the weather was hot. That
Tennessee State Capitol was like a sauna inside. That sure
seemed to fuel the short tempers of the legislators, who
had come together in a special session to debate the constitutional amendment before them. And *debate* is a nice
word for what was going on . . . because for days and days
they argued, fought, yelled, and tried to influence the
other side. But they were still deadlocked.

At twenty-four years old, Harry Burn was the youngest
representative in state legislature, and as it happened, his
vote was crucial. Representatives had to make a decision
that would change history—not only for Tennessee, but
also for the United States. You see, thirty-five states had already ratified the amendment they were debating, and
one more would make it law. The amendment would be

added to the Constitution of the United States. The anti-ratification folks all wore red roses on their lapels. The pro-ratification side wore yellow roses. Harry Burn . . . wore a red rose. So why was he hiding in the attic of the Capitol with his own red-rose-wearing allies out to get his blood?

Well, hang on, we're getting to that! All of a sudden the red-rose-wearing Speaker of the House moved to table the amendment, which would have buried it. But the table vote was a tie and the Speaker had no choice but to call the measure to a ratification vote. One by one, the members called out their choices.

Aye.

Nay.

They all sweltered in the stifling heat . . . and worried. The vote was going to be close. In the midst of all this . . . a messenger arrived with a telegram for Harry. The telegram had a yellow rose attached to it. It was from Harry's mother back in Niota, Tennessee. She had been reading about the speeches in the newspapers and was offering some advice. Harry agonized over the decision before him. His resolve was wavering. What would he do? His colleagues expected his support, but his mother had always given him good advice.

Then it was time to vote. When they called Harry's name he voiced a resounding "aye!" Upon hearing this unexpected change in Harry's vote, the Speaker also changed his vote and the amendment was ratified by the slimmest of margins.

Just what could make a young man take his life in his hands to cast such an unpopular vote? Harry said later, "I know that a mother's advice is always best for her boy to follow, and my mother wanted me to vote for ratification."

Yes, it's a little-known fact that in 1920 a mother from a tiny town in Tennessee was the deciding factor in influencing her son Harry to change his vote and thereby ratify a constitutional amendment . . . giving women the right to vote. A mother's advice is never wasted!

LITTLE-KNOWN FACT #31

The Actor Who Didn't Talk

For Archie, life started out hard. Then it got harder. He was born in an English slum to a neurotic, unstable mother and a magic father. Archie called him Magic, because he was always disappearing, frequently for days on end.

And they were poor. Dirt poor. He had no clothes. His mother dressed him in . . . dresses until he was nine years old. That's when he got his first pair of trousers.

But one thing was certain: He was talented. Everyone saw it, especially his teachers in school and his soccer coach. Archie was the best goalie in his school. That earned him some respect, but no money. And Archie wanted money. At age sixteen he tried out as a stand-in for a traveling road show. He got the part. Several months later, the show wound up in Manhattan—New York. He thought he had it made, until he came down with rheumatic fever. The show moved on and left Archie behind.

He recovered, but he was still broke and now three thousand miles from home and unemployed. He took a job as a sandwich-board advertising man—some of you may remember them, boys who wore big boards on both sides of their bodies advertising a local store or eatery—

except Archie had to do his bit on nine-foot stilts and Coney Island's famous boardwalk.

Well, as soon as he could he tried out for more shows, this time on Broadway. And he got several parts—all of them nonspeaking. They said he talked funny. Nobody wanted to hear his funny accent. But he had grown into a handsome fellow . . . and he could play to the audience with his eyes . . . and he did. He was known as the actor who didn't talk. Three years, five different plays, nine different roles, over five hundred performances—and he'd never spoken on stage. Still, it was money, and he was doing what he wanted to do.

Finally one day in 1927, during a show for Oscar Hammerstein's *"Golden Dawn,"* he said his first words on stage . . . and nothing has been the same since. Audiences fell in love with Archie and Archie with them.

It's a little-known fact that the man who was not allowed to utter a word on stage because he "talked funny" went on to become one of the world's greatest leading men. Archibald Leach. You might know him as . . . Cary Grant!

LITTLE-KNOWN FACT #32

The Dedicated Hero

Alfred saw the sun glinting off a rifle barrel in a stand of trees. He knew sniper fire was coming. He grabbed his commander, Major Donovan, and covered the major's body with his own—even as the sniper's bullets cut Alfred down.

He was mortally wounded, but he didn't die right

away. He was taken to the field hospital, where everyone learned of his incredible bravery and how he saved his commander's life.

And as he lay dying, he thought of his wife and children back in New York. He could have stayed home. He didn't have to enlist. But that wasn't the kind of man Alfred was. The United States had just entered World War I, and he felt it was his duty—almost a sacred duty, as he put it—to help make the world safe for democracy. He was assigned to the 165th Infantry and, since he was a college graduate, was made the regimental statistician. But it wasn't too long before Alfred's unit was sent to France.

Once there, he very quickly rose to the rank of sergeant and was assigned to the newly organized regimental intelligence staff. He was made an observer, and if you think that sounds like someone who sits around and watches what's happening, well, that's not quite what Alfred did. What he did do was go on night patrols through the heart of no-man's-land, gathering information of tactical importance to his regiment and his division. It was an incredibly dangerous assignment—and incredibly productive. He brought back vital data for his superiors.

The upside of Alfred's job as an observer is that he didn't have any front-line duties during actual combat. But you've probably figured out by now that that didn't stop Alfred. He told his superiors that he absolutely would not be kept out of action while his comrades were at risk. And so it happened on a hot July day in 1918, at the Battle of the Ourcq, that Alfred attached himself as adjutant to Major William Donovan, the commander of the first battalion, right in the thick of things.

The very day before, Donovan's last adjutant had been killed in combat. But Alfred was by his side as the battle was joined again. The enemy fire came closer and closer to their position, but Alfred never wavered, always watching out for his commanding officer. Now lying here in a field hospital, mortally wounded, his thoughts drifted back to those things he cherished and loved.

His family . . . and nature, for he'd always been a lover of the natural beauty of the outdoors.

In fact, if we remember Alfred today, it's not for his heroism in World War I, but for his keen observations of the natural world. It's a little-known fact that the man who showed such exceptional bravery in the face of battle is the same man who wrote the now-famous words, "I think that I shall never see / a poem lovely as a tree." Hero. Poet. Alfred Joyce Kilmer.

LITTLE-KNOWN FACT #33

The Trailblazer

You know, when you're the first at anything, there's going to be problems. And I guess it really doesn't matter what it is that you're first at. Some people will hate you, others will love you . . . and there will be that big bunch of folks who just kind of sit back and watch carefully, to see what you are all about.

I guess that was probably true with Charles Lindbergh. He was hailed as the first person to fly to Atlantic Ocean nonstop. But news reports tell us that a bunch of people thought it was wrong to do it. And another bunch just didn't believe it at all.

That also happened when Neil Armstrong first stepped

foot on the moon. The day he took off, there were people at Cape Canaveral protesting the launch. And still today, there are people who believe that the entire space program is a government plot . . . .and that we never have flown into space. Columbus faced it when he found the New World. People scoffed at Newton and laughed at Darwin. It's always a tough road to be first. Like it was for the first player in the major leagues who was different. You know . . . he wasn't a white player. He was black. Things were a little different back then, as I'm sure you know. He couldn't always stay in the same hotels or eat in the same restaurants as the other players on the team. As a matter of fact, he seldom could. He often had to ride in a separate part of the train when they traveled. And according to him, he actually ran into more of that kind of discrimination in the North than he did in the South. He wasn't sure why. He thought that people in the North would be more understanding and liberal about those attitudes—after all, that was why they fought the Civil War. The North won and freed the slaves. Or so he thought.

But no.

According to Bud, the discrimination was far worse in the North than when he played in the South. Who's Bud, you ask? Oh, that would be Bud Fowler. The first black ballplayer ever to play in the major leagues. Confused? I don't blame you, the way our news media writes history.

But it's a little-known fact that Bud Fowler was the first black player to ever play on an American League team, out of Chicago. And he did so almost forty years before Jackie Robinson first set foot on a ball diamond. But in order to play, Bud had to pass himself off as an Indian. It's a shame. We know better now, though, and he still doesn't get the credit.

LITTLE-KNOWN FACT #34

The Great Swindle

You know, things aren't always the way they appear. And if you've been listening to our little show for very long, then you've also learned that history doesn't always record things in a proper perspective. And that may be the case with Peter Minuit. The year was 1626, and Peter was the director general of a small colony owned by the Dutch West India Company on what is now Manhattan Island, New York.

Remember, this was four hundred years ago. Shoot, it took months to have any kind of correspondence with his home office in Amsterdam. So his authority on the island was absolute! What Peter said went in the little colony, without question.

For those of you who have been there, you know that today Manhattan is one of the busiest and most populated places on earth. But in 1626, it was just a little island on the edge of vast undiscovered continent. Still, Peter decided that this little piece of real estate was vital to his company interest in the New World—which by the way was called New Amsterdam back then—and he was going to secure it once and for all.

You know what happened next. Peter got together with the Canarsie Indians and negotiated a price of twenty-four dollars for the entire island. A seemingly paltry sum. But by today's standards, it's the equivalent to a million dollars.

Now, history has recorded for all time that Peter cheated

the Canarsie out of one of the most precious pieces of real estate in the world. But it's a little-known fact that the Canarsie were far savvier than we've been led to believe.

You see, when Peter made his now-famous deal to purchase Manhattan, the Canarsie Indians didn't own or even occupy the island. They lived somewhere else. The Canarsie never did consider Manhattan a part of their territory. But they were smart enough to take Peter's money—even though Manhattan Island was never theirs to sell.

LITTLE-KNOWN FACT #35

The Tailor

If you were a young man seeking a fortune back in the late 1840s, then west to the gold fields of California was the way you went.

We know that Jacob Davis did.

But Jacob didn't go all the way to the West Coast. He stopped just short of the Sierra Mountains, in the high desert of Nevada. Perhaps he liked the desert, or maybe he saw an opportunity where he did stop, and saw no need to go any farther. In any case, he set up shop in Nevada.

Here, gold wasn't king—silver was. Yes, believe it or not, there was a silver rush going on almost simultaneously with the more famous gold rush in California. And Jacob, well, he found himself right in the middle of it all. Jacob did go west to seek his fortune, but he wasn't going to dig in the earth. No, he'd let other people do that. But Jacob did know a lot of miners, of course, and they were often coming to him for help, with torn shirts, pants worn out from days on their hands and knees, digging, scraping, washing the ore. They came to him, you see, because Jacob was a tailor. You might say that he was tailor to the Nevada silver miners and prospectors.

And let me tell you, Jacob was busy. Very busy! You see, mining is tough work, on the men and their clothes. Mining clothes, especially pants, were constantly in need of repair or replacing. There were no off-the-shelf clothes made in those days. And Jacob started to tinker with better ways to make them. He was also interested in figuring out ways of making them so that they would survive the grinding work of the miner.

He managed to find a particularly rugged cloth being sold at a new store in San Francisco. That store was in the business of selling supplies to the California gold rush miners—and the store's owners were getting rich at it, I might add. Well, Jacob wasn't getting rich. He was doing all right, but tailors never did make tremendous amounts of money. That was especially true for tailors who made clothes for the workingmen of those days.

But Jacob figured he'd discovered a new way to make work pants, figured it might even be worth a patent, but he didn't have the money or the time to pursue it. So in 1873, he struck a deal with the San Francisco store owner who was supplying him with the bolts of brown duck and indigo blue cloth. Jacob asked him if he would initiate the paperwork for filing a patent. Suggested that they could then go into business together producing the new pants. And it almost happened that way.

You see, it's a little-known fact that Jacob Davis invented blue jeans, and the store owner—Levi Strauss—put up the money and the paperwork to file for the patent. So the next time you think about wearing your Levi's, just think: Maybe they should have been called Jacob's instead.

LITTLE-KNOWN FACT #36

Giving Heroes a Hand

The young policeman was nervous. He had good reason to be. The angry armed robber was holding the elderly lady in front of him as he moved out of the bank to the waiting car.

Slowly, carefully, the young policeman stood up from his position behind his patrol car and moved toward the desperate man and the terrified lady. It was a brave thing to do—but he knew he had an ace in the hole.

Suddenly, the nervous young punk pushed the lady aside and ran for the car, taking a shot at the approaching policeman. The shot was accurate; the bullet caught the brave young officer in the middle of his chest.

He felt the strong thump from the bullet and then dived to cover the old woman, now crouching on the ground. In one sure, swift motion, he took a shot at the fleeing robber—and his aim was perfect. He caught him in the back of the leg, just enough to bring him down, enough time for the other policemen on the scene to rush in, kick the gun from his hand, throw him to the ground, and end the deadly episode.

The nerve-racking scene was just one of hundreds that are played out every day as the police try to keep us safe from criminals. And these brave men in uniform are able to make that courageous move because—well, because S. L. Kwolek did not have enough money for medical school.

Kwolek was born in Pennsylvania in 1923 and knew tough times right from the get-go. You see, the senior Kwolek died just a few years later, and his wife was left to raise the two children by herself, just as the Depression was beginning.

Despite the tough times, Mrs. Kwolek made sure that her children got an education. S. L. even managed to get a degree from college in 1946 and was hoping to go to medical school. But there was no money. However, there was a job up at the DuPont company in Buffalo, New York.

Which is where the young graduate not only went to work, but went on to excel in the company. Among the many inventions credited to S. L. Kwolek is an amazing fiber that is five times stronger than steel.

This versatile fiber, called Kevlar, is used in radial tires, racing sails, fiber-optic cable, spacecraft shells, bridge suspension cables . . . and Kevlar is also the stuff inside a policeman's bulletproof vest.

It's a little known fact that because S. L.—Stephanie Louise—Kwolek did not have enough money for medical school, she went on to become one of top women inventors of the twentieth century.

LITTLE-KNOWN FACT #37

FBI Case Number 145-2961

Where do legends come from? Well, usually they evolve from older legends, as people tell them again and again.

And maybe that's the case here. And I say *case*, because that's what it was. A criminal case, officially FBI Case #145-2961.

They were investigating the interstate transport of obscene material. It was getting so much attention that even the FBI's esteemed director and noted strongman, J. Edgar Hoover himself, was involved and monitoring every step of the investigation.

The only problem was, they couldn't find it—the obscene material, that is. The FBI was sure that it was there; they had it from the best sources, and they were going to prove it, then arrest the offending culprits. But first they had to find the offensive material and so far, they had been unable to do so. The FBI even hired outside experts to help provide evidence and bring this awful case to trial, but the experts failed, too.

You may find this hard to believe, but what had the FBI and J. Edgar himself all riled up was a song. The song was written by Richard Berry in 1957, and had been recorded several times in the next couple of years. But no one paid any attention to it—that is, until a new rock-and-roll group picked it up and made it their lead song on a new album.

As you know, bands traditionally put their lyrics on the album jacket so the fans can sing along, too. But in this case the band thought the lyrics were kind of simplistic and, well, mushy . . . so they left them off the cover. Oh, they did one other thing, too: They thought the album would sell better if the fan couldn't understand the silly lyrics, so the band mumbled the words.

That's all it took! The FBI saw something inherently evil about that act and launched a five-year investigation. And you know what? They never did find anything obscene. At least not in the original version.

Well, it's a little-known fact that this one song has been recorded over twelve hundred times by such artists as Otis Redding, Little Richard, Barry White, Paul Revere and the Raiders, Beau Brummell, and many more.

It is one of the most recorded songs in history and the truth is, that it's nothing more than a simple ditty about a Jamaican sailor who's away from home and thinking about his girlfriend. But nobody ever really knew what the lyrics were. And almost every band that ever recorded the song . . . made up what they thought they heard. No one ever sang the real lyrics to "Louie Louie."

LITTLE-KNOWN FACT #38

Lincoln's Choice

Abraham Lincoln knew that this would be one of his most important decisions. The storm clouds of war were gathering and the fate of the country was in the balance.

The president knew that the man he chose to lead the Union army had to be just the right man. So he called upon someone who was known as the smartest man in the U.S. Army. A man whose reputation as a brilliant strategist went as far back as his days at the military academy.

The general whom Lincoln sent for was a man of letters—a man who would write beautiful and moving letters to his mother, and later, to the mothers of the men who were lost in the great Civil War of America.

When he was growing up, he knew that destiny awaited him in some fashion. That there would be some call he would have to answer. He would later write in his diaries of his solitary hunting trips through the snowy winters when he would spend many hours alone, contemplating his life and his future.

One chapter in his diary describes how he would sometimes follow the hounds through the snow-covered hills on foot all day. Many of the books later written about him would describe his great strength and endurance. His adventures as an energetic, curious boy would prepare him well for the ordeal ahead.

Even when he was a boy, he wanted only to be a soldier. Little did he know that his ideas about how to fight a war would later become legendary. How could he have imagined that his campaigns in America's great war would be universally studied in military schools as models of strategy and tactics?

He was very moved when he was told the president of the United States wanted to see him. When he arrived at the White House, Lincoln complimented him on his outstanding record and well-known reputation as the best general in the army.

Lincoln told him that war was now inevitable. No matter how many times he had appealed to the reason and wisdom of the southern statesmen, they could not agree.

There was a great battle coming. Would he take command and lead the Union armies in order to save the country? America's best soldier thought for a moment and then told Lincoln, no, he could not.

It is a little-known fact that the first general that Abraham Lincoln asked to lead the Union army was General Robert E. Lee.

LITTLE-KNOWN FACT #39

The Speechifiers

If the truth were told, any one of us might make a pretty good president. But most of us probably wouldn't have enough get-up-and-go to even get elected.

Think about it a minute.

Anybody running for president has to show up everywhere. And say a whole bunch to whoever wants to listen. Now, an ordinary person might find the whole thing exhausting, but it takes a lot to slow down a guy running for president. Just consider Teddy Roosevelt.

In 1912 he found himself in Milwaukee, campaigning for president again. He'd already served two terms, but after four years out of office, he wanted back in. Just minutes before he was scheduled to speak to a big crowd of voters, he was shot. Lucky for him, he was carrying his eyeglass case and a fifty-page speech in his breast pocket. This absorbed a lot of the force of the bullet . . . but it still lodged in his chest, somewhere close to his lung.

Now that must have hurt! And Roosevelt, well, he was dripping with blood when he stumbled up to the podium.

"Please excuse me," he told the crowd, "from making a long speech . . . there's a bullet in my body."

But even that wasn't enough to stop him. "I have a message to deliver, and I will deliver it as long as there is life in my body," he assured the crowd.

Well, there was plenty of life in him yet. After all, he spoke for an hour and a half. Even though he did have to wing it a time or two, seeing as how there was a large bullet hole ripping though the pages of the speech he was trying to read.

Speech making must be some kind of calling. Because even when some of the candidates finally did get to be president, they still make a whole lot of them. Probably the most important speech to presidents is their first one, the one they make on the day of their inauguration.

It was so important to Lyndon B. Johnson that he hired twenty-four speechwriters to work on his. It took them six weeks and sixteen revisions to come up with a three-thousand-word draft that passed Lyndon's strict requirements.

Americans witnessed the longest inauguration speech in history in 1841. That year crowds had to shiver through a snowstorm to hear William Henry Harrison swear to do his best for his country. William kept his audience out in the cold with a speech that was almost nine thousand words long. He stood on that freezing March day and spoke eloquently on a multitude of subjects. In his best suit, without a hat or a coat. For two long hours. But it sure cost him.

It's a little-known fact that Harrison didn't have near the stamina that Teddy did. One month from that day, William Harrison died . . . from pneumonia. And so it was that he went down in history as having the longest inaugural speech—and the shortest term—of any U.S. president.

LITTLE-KNOWN FACT #40

Accept No Imitations!

As far as I can tell, none of us gets much say-so when it comes to the time and place of our own birth. Looks to me like most of us just come on into this world and work things out the best we can. But if we *could* choose—well now, things might work out a lot differently for some of us. Take Elijah, for instance. I bet if we could ask him, he sure wouldn't have chosen to be born in 1844, the son of two former slaves who escaped from Kentucky to Canada on the Underground Railroad. After that dangerous journey to the Canadian border, Elijah's dad helped defend his new country in the Rebel War of 1837. It won him a land grant and the right to send his children to school.

Elijah's folks knew early on that their son had more than his share of talent when it came to anything mechanical . . . and when he turned sixteen, they had saved enough to send him to Edinburgh, Scotland, to train to be an engineer. By the time Elijah finished school, he was a master mechanic and engineer . . . and the Civil War had come and gone in America. So he settled in Michigan, a free, educated man. The only trouble was, most Americans had never heard of an educated black person. So Elijah had a hard time finding work. He finally took a job as a fire- and oilman for the Michigan Central Railroad. It probably looked to him like all those years of education would go to waste.

Think back to those times . . . the job of a fireman was to scoop coal into the firebox that kept the engine running. Every hour, Elijah had to shovel about two tons of coal into that box—and keep it up all day long. And every few miles the train would stop and Elijah would walk the entire length of the train, oiling the axles, bearings, and other moving parts on each car. Then he would race back to the cab and start in shoveling coal. Now, Elijah was a smart man and he knew there had to be an easier way. So for two years he worked on a special lubricating cup that would automatically drip oil when it was needed. In 1872, he patented his first model.

Officials of the Michigan Central Railroad recognized the ingenuity of Elijah's invention and let him install them on every train they had. It didn't take people long to see how well they worked. This discovery alone allowed Elijah to quit the hard life on the railroad and take to inventing full time. You've heard of the lawn sprinkler and ironing board, haven't you? Well you can thank Elijah for those. Even today his inventions are used in construction, factories, naval boats, and even space exploration vehicles. But it was those lubricating cups that really changed his life. Now, you know how it goes when any good invention hits the market: About a hundred copycats come out with their own, slightly different model . . . but nobody wanted those knock-offs. Everybody in the train business knew to ask for Elijah's device by name.

And yes, even you've heard the common phrase that their many requests helped make famous. It's a phrase that many say originated with a Captain Bill who ran bootleg whiskey into the United States during Prohibition.

But it's a little-known fact that some fifty years earlier, engineers asked a single question when they were looking to outfit their trains . . . and it was the same one that years later customers would ask Captain Bill. Is it, they wondered, the real McCoy?

Well, I don't know about the whiskey, but if they were looking at one of the first inventions by an African American named Elijah McCoy, it certainly was.

LITTLE-KNOWN FACT #41

Real Miners Don't Drink Tea

It wasn't all that long ago that oil was still just a curse in the West. That dark, gruesome stuff could be pure poison to water supplies. The idea that this black goo would one day fuel the world—well, most old-timers would have gotten quite a chuckle out of that one!

Back then, coal was king. And way up until the middle of the nineteenth century we were still a nation that pretty much depended on it. And on the miners who spent their days a thousand feet underground digging it up.

Now, those coal miners, they weren't ordinary men . . . no, not by a long shot. Thousands of laborers worked in the mines, but only a handful of them had the stuff to be a miner. It was work for craftsmen. Chucking coal out of solid rock was no easy task. Not only did it take a certain amount of skill, but anybody who tried it had to be uncommonly strong to succeed. Even the tools a miner carried around would tax most of us. A single pickax could weigh up to ten pounds, and many a miner carried several different types of them. And then there was the danger. And quite a lot of that, too. In just the thirty years between 1870 and 1900, at least ten thousand men and boys were killed in America's coal mines. And more than twenty-five thousand were hurt so badly that they were lucky to ever work again. And forget about worker's comp. Nobody had heard of that yet.

It's no wonder that coal miners acquired a certain reputation. Citizens just naturally treated them with respect. And usually gave them a wide berth. Now, the one thing miners did as hard as they worked, was drink. In the coal-mining towns of Pennsylvania, it's said that saloons accounted for more than half of the businesses in town. The mining community of Homestead might have had only seventy thousand residents, but at least fifty saloons and speakeasies lined the main streets. And with all these saloons came competition. Alcohol was dirt cheap. Gambling and prostitution, crime and killing all increased, too.

It wasn't long before it came to the attention of some that America, for all its graces, had a drinking problem.

By the 1870s, temperance movements had swept across the nation. The Anti-Saloon League and the Women's Crusade gained so much momentum that, within thirty years, the entire country would be dry. But in Pennsylvania, the miners had the temperance workers worried. So worried, in fact, that the Reverend Russell Cornwell, founder of Temple University and a temperance man himself, knew something would have to be done about these hard, hard cases. So he talked a pharmacist friend he knew into cooking up something. But it would have to be something mighty powerful to convince these miners to quit the liquor they loved.

Well, Charlie the pharmacist poured, measured, experimented—much like any good chemist—until he had quite a concoction on his hands. His new find listed in its ingredients anywhere from sixteen to twenty-three wild roots—licorice, wintergreen, juniper . . . a few berries and even the bark from a tree!

He brewed it much as you would a tea and added a few things, like vanilla and honey, to cut back on the bite. But it still packed quite a punch for a tea. Charlie lost no time in trying to sell it to those hard-core miners. Well, wouldn't you know it, real miners didn't drink tea. And Charlie's attempts to entice them from their saloons was a total flop.

But then Dr. Cromwell gave Charlie a piece of sage advice. And it proved to change the outcome of things. It's a little-known fact that Charlie switched the name of his exotic new drink from a *tea* to a *beer*, and it took off like a rocket. In fact, this new brew kept the beer factories from going out of business during the long years of Prohibition. You've probably guessed it: Instead of wild root tea, Charles Hires sold his original draft root beer . . . and miners everywhere were proud to drink it.

LITTLE-KNOWN FACT #42

The Angel of Mercy

Clarisse Harlow had done and seen a lot of things in her life, but nothing had prepared her for this. This was just a little more than she expected. She'd thought the job would be tough and fraught with dangers, but this was much more. Clarisse was a field nurse with the Union army during the Civil War. She was in places like Fredericksburg and Antietam. The wounded were everywhere. Sometimes it seemed that she couldn't get away from it no matter how far from the front she was.

But when she was at the front, which she was frequently, it was . . . well, war! At Fredericksburg, with the battle in full rage less than half a mile away, she stepped outside the medical tent for a breath of fresh air. She had just been tending to a soldier who had had his leg blown off, and she dearly needed to escape the smell of blood for just a minute. She noticed a large group of civilians on the other side of a fence just a few yards away. She was shocked to see civilians so close to the battle lines. The people started shouting at her, and she went a little closer.

Clarisse realized they were shouting out names, the names of their husbands and sons and brothers, wanting to know where they were, whether they were alive or dead. She told them that she didn't have any of that information. But she would never forget the look in the eyes of those relatives . . . wondering if they still had a brother, or husband, or father.

The pain of those people, from just plain not knowing, was an image so powerful that it kept her awake night after night and even stayed with her long after the war was over. One day, she heard that there were thousands of soldiers still unaccounted for. So she decided to do something about it.

Clarisse went to the old Confederate prison camp at Andersonville, Georgia, where more than thirteen thousand Union prisoners had been held. Many of them had died there, and lay in unmarked graves. She made a list of the missing, and set about trying to get a list of the prisoners who'd been there. She compared the two, and within a few months, she was able to tell literally thousands of families where their loved ones were buried.

Word got around about what Clarisse had done, and people all over the country sent her letters with the names of their family members. She published her lists in the newspapers. She made flyers to put up in post offices everywhere, from Maine to Texas. She worked almost nonstop for three years finding the soldiers. The U.S. government was so impressed that they established an office of missing soldiers—headed by Clarisse Harlow. She became the first woman to ever lead a government agency. By the time she was finished, Clarisse had located more than twenty-two thousand missing soldiers. Right now you might be asking, Why have I never heard of a woman who did so much good?

Oh, you have. Because she went on to do even more. It's a little-known fact that the woman who was our first missing person locator and was the first woman to lead a government agency was the same woman who founded the American Red Cross: Clara Harlow Barton.

LITTLE-KNOWN FACT #43

His Majesty's Soldiers Meet the American . . . Rowdies?

If you want to know who the rowdiest rebels were during the American Revolution, just take a look at Massachusetts. When Samuel Adams and the Sons of Liberty dressed up like Indians and dumped 343 chests full of tea into Boston Harbor, well, it was business as usual for these guys. But I guess it did make the British a sight madder than they had been. They closed down the harbor and swore they'd stomp out this rebellion in a matter of days.

Now, the truth is, the British really weren't too worried about the colonial uprising. They thought all they had to do was send out a ship or two and the rebels would turn tail and run. Royal officers told their troops that the colonials were "raw, undisciplined, cowardly men."

"The very sound of a cannon will carry them off," they boasted.

To the British, these "urban rowdies" were just a bunch of smugglers, some buckskin-wearing frontiersmen, and a few deadbeat southern planters. And Sam Adams, John Hancock, and the other leaders of the Massachusetts rebellion, well they were downright criminals . . . fit only to hang.

It was probably the day after Paul Revere took his ride through the countryside that the English first lost a bit of their cocky attitude. On April 19, 1775. The very day that the famous shot was heard around the world. British troops suffered their first defeat at the Battle of Concord. Fact is, the American revolutionaries were so mad they chased the British all the way from Concord, up through Lexington and straight back to Boston.

But that wasn't the only lesson the British learned that day, not by a long shot. If England had wanted to know how hard these ragtag soldiers would be to defeat, all they had to do was look closely at the squabble at Menotomy, a small settlement about an hour's march from Lexington. It so happens that a convoy of British soldiers on their way to join the main regiment took a wrong turn somewhere. And they came up against twelve old men who had been left to defend that village.

To the surprise of the British, these ancient warriors opened fire.

The English soldiers who didn't fall in that first volley of muskets turned and ran through town, throwing their arms into a passing pond. They eventually ran into an old woman digging dandelions in her garden. And to her they surrendered. It's a little-known fact that the first prisoners of the American Revolution were the trophy of Mother Batherick, a grandmother many times over.

LITTLE-KNOWN FACT #44

The Story of Nancy Green

Ouch. It was that sound you hate to hear, folks: the squeal of automobile brakes and then a muffled thump and somebody falling to the ground.

A lot of people ran over to see if they could help the elderly lady lying in the street. But it was too late. Nancy Green was dead. The strange thing was, though, that most of the people in the crowd recognized her. They didn't know her, didn't know her name, but they recognized her.

And the same thing happened at the hospital and then at the funeral home. Whenever anybody looked at the face of the old woman, they were positive that, somehow, they knew who she was.

Nancy Green was born in Kentucky. As a little girl, the thing she loved the most was to watch her mama cooking. She quickly picked up all of her mama's techniques and became quite a good cook herself.

She moved from Kentucky to Chicago, and that's where she met Mr. Christopher Rutt, a newspaperman. Now, Chris was all excited because he had just found a new product that he was sure would just take off and make him a million dollars in no time at all.

One of the things he needed was somebody to represent him and show people how good this new stuff was. So he hired Nancy Green. Nancy would demonstrate his product to the visitors at the 1893 World's Fair in Chicago. And man, was she a hit. She not only had a genuine skill for cooking, but her warm and appealing personality made her presentation the most popular booth at the fair. Hundreds of people would gather around her booth just to watch Nancy prepare this new product.

They even had to hire police to keep the crowds moving. The fair officials ended up awarding her a medal for her showmanship.

And as you might imagine, Chris Rutt was a happy man. He got over fifty thousand orders from Nancy Green's presentation alone. She was so good that he gave her a lifetime contract. She went on to represent him for the next thirty years.

The product she demonstrated at the fair did take off, just as Chris hoped it would. Nancy Green traveled the entire country for years introducing millions of folks to this new idea that soon became one of America's most popular foods.

It is a little-known fact that the eighty-nine-year-old Nancy Green, who was born a slave, and who was killed by a car on the South Side of Chicago, had been known for thirty years, as Aunt Jemima.

LITTLE-KNOWN FACT #45

Lenin's Warning

Do you remember the Peter Principle? That's the theory that you get promoted to your level of incompetence.

Well, a lot of folks joke that government is a breeding ground for that kind of thing. Then every so often something happens that proves . . . it's not so funny! Like that night on April 11, 1917, when a young duty officer at the American legation in Berne, Switzerland, sat daydreaming about a certain social engagement he had later that evening. Now, this was right in the middle of World War I, and his duty post was one of great importance. At least it should have been, if he had not been so intent on his social life. Because late that afternoon his telephone rang. It was a man with a deep German accent who identified himself as the central figure in the Russian Revolution.

It was none other than I. V. Lenin himself.

Lenin was trying to deliver an important message about the war to the Americans. The Bolsheviks had overthrown the Russian czar just a few days before, and Lenin, who liked President Woodrow Wilson, wanted to pass along some vital information that he knew would affect the American war effort. When our young duty officer answered the phone, Lenin said he had some extremely important information and that he needed to speak with someone at the delegation. The young man asked if it couldn't wait until tomorrow during regular hours.

"No!" Lenin told the young man. "This is urgent business concerning the war and tomorrow will be too late!"

The young officer on duty thought it over: "What could be so important that it couldn't wait until tomorrow morning?" Besides an urgent message right now would certainly interrupt his plans for the evening. Anyway, this man with the German accent was probably just some crackpot. Whatever it was, it certainly didn't merit canceling his date with a beautiful woman.

Now, you may find this hard to believe, but that young duty officer told Lenin he would have to wait until the next morning at 10 A.M. when the office opened for regular hours. You might guess what Lenin's reaction was. If the Americans didn't care . . . then why should he? So Lenin talked to no one. And six days later Russia pulled out of World War I, leaving the entire Eastern Front unguarded.

Now, most people would have thought that was a very important message indeed. But wait till you hear what happened to that young duty officer who dropped the ball. It's a little-known fact that the young officer who refused to break his date to meet with Lenin was Allen Dulles . . . the future head of the CIA.

LITTLE-KNOWN FACT #46

Oops!

For Norma Talmadge it may have been Christmas, but there was little joy at home. For this was the day that Fred, her alcoholic and unemployed father, decided to leave Norma's mother, Peg, and her two sisters to fend for themselves. Yes, things seemed dire at the time—a woman left alone back in the early 1900s: There just weren't many career opportunities. And the New Jersey winters were cold.

But Peg was strong willed. She took in laundry to support her family. She was a good role model for her daughters, and at the age of fourteen, Norma took a modeling job to help out. Truth be told, Norma was a bit stagestruck. She was a beautiful girl with dark brown hair and eyes, and it wasn't long before she was discovered and began a film career with Vita-graph Studio. Her first appearance in films wasn't exactly a leading role—only the back of her head showed—but Norma worked hard and within five years she had appeared in more than a hundred films and increased her salary tenfold. Vita-graph got its money's worth out of Norma, and it was there that Norma learned the business inside and out. She not only played everything from a teenager to a grandma, she also assisted with costuming and makeup.

Finally, Norma got her big break and was offered a contract out in Hollywood. Norma's chance to become a successful Hollywood actress was also her mother Peg's chance to become the quintessential stage mother. By this time, the entire family was stagestruck, including sisters Constance and Natalie. In fact, when Norma's film flopped and the studio shut down, it was Constance who got her another contract. Norma made good on that contract and starred in several films. But when the contract ran out, she decided to step out on her own.

It was about the same time Norma fell in love and got married. And so it was that Norma and her new husband started their own production company. Again, Norma was a success. She became one of the glamorous Hollywood stars. But history will probably remember Norma more for being clumsy than glamorous and starting one of Hollywood's biggest traditions.

It's a little-known fact that at a gala grand opening of one of her films young and lovely Norma Talmadge stumbled and fell into some wet cement outside Grauman's Chinese Theatre, leaving the very first set of movie star's handprints.

LITTLE-KNOWN FACT #47

Old Kinderhook

Few historians would argue that Martin Van Buren was one of our most unsuccessful presidents—except for one thing. You may not know, for example, that Martin was the first of our presidents to be born a U.S. citizen. All the rest were born before we became a country and had citizenship.

But that wasn't something he did, of course.

Although he was all American, his parents spoke Dutch. And they stubbornly held on to their Dutch language a hundred years after the British had taken New York. So Martin grew up on a big estate in upstate New York that went back in the family. He called the estate Old Kinderhook, and believe it or not, it wasn't long before people started referring to Martin himself as Old Kinderhook.

Martin parlayed his personal skills and his private fortune into a position as a power broker in New York State. In those days senators were elected by the state legislature, so it was natural for Martin to be elected to the U.S. Senate in 1821.

Now, Martin was nothing if he wasn't a clever politician, and he could see a star rising from a long way off. Long before Andy Jackson became president of the United States, Martin promoted him to his fellow New Yorkers, which helped a lot in getting Jackson elected. As a reward, Andrew Jackson appointed Martin his secretary of state, the most prestigious position in the cabinet.

Four years later, because of Martin's loyal service, Jackson asked him to run as his vice president for his second term and, of course, Andy Jackson was reelected. Then in 1836, Martin was elected president in his own right.

By this time he had been in the White House a long time and, as I said, he was known to all his friends and foes alike by his nickname, Old Kinderhook. You might guess then when he became president, he didn't sign his name to pieces of legislation or to policy statements he approved. Oh no. Whenever Martin signed off on something, he signed it Old Kinderhook, even though President Martin Van Buren presided over the first American depression and didn't know what to do about it, and even though he angered abolitionists in the North and was defeated for reelection by General William Henry Harrison, he had one lasting success. And that was the way he signed his name . . . Old Kinderhook.

It's a little-known fact that Martin van Buren is responsible for a word that is used more than any other in the entire world today. You see, when he signed Old Kinderhook, he just used his initials. And getting the official OK on a document started the most universal of all words.

Got it?

Okay!

LITTLE-KNOWN FACT #48

Lost Woman

The year was 1850, and it was in the cooler month of October, in the Nebraska territories, that a group of travelers boarded a stagecoach for the three-week trip to the Oregon territory. The three men and one woman were engaged in some friendly chat when, a couple of hours into the trip, the coach slowed and stopped.

There on the side of the road was an old Indian woman. Passenger B. J. Cummings remembers his first glimpse of her. Cummings, a banker headed west to open a new bank, wrote in his diary that "lost woman" was very spry. That's how the driver greeted her, by the name of Lost Woman. She got into the coach as comfortably as if she had done it a dozen times . . . and indeed she had. She was a regular on the line, traveling back and forth across much of the Dakota and Nebraska territories.

Whether the other passengers minded her being there we don't know, but we do know that a few miles down the road she would prove herself indispensable. The stage hadn't gone very far when the driver pulled up short again. Three armed men on horseback stood blocking the road. All the passengers were ordered out of the stage, robbed, and left on the side of the road. The bandits took off with their money, their valuables, and the stagecoach, too.

They were thirty miles from the nearest stage depot. Ginny Long didn't think she could make the walk, much less be able to dodge the bandits, hostile Indians, and any other scoundrels they might encounter along the way. And they had no food, no water, and no shelter. Lost Woman told the passengers to stay where they were; she would be back with help soon. She left, and the other passengers were sure they had seen the last of her.

When the second day broke and Lost Woman had still not returned, they started estimating their chances of making it on their own. Just about the time that they had decided to try walking to the next stop, Lost Woman showed up with about ten other Indians, fresh horses, food, and water. They were taken to the next stage depot and sent on their way. They thanked Lost Woman for literally saving their lives.

But it wasn't until they heard one of the other Indians address the woman in her own language that they realized who she was, and that saving lives was nothing new to this special woman. It's a little-known fact that Lost Woman had performed similar feats of heroism most of her life. In fact, nearly forty-five years earlier she had done the same thing for the very first group of white men to ever come through the area: the famed scouting and mapping mission of Meriwether Lewis and William Clark. And the woman who was now called Lost Woman was, indeed, none other than Sacagawea herself.

LITTLE-KNOWN FACT #49

The Old Codger

War is hell. And I mean that literally. Jaynes knew it. He was in the middle of it. He was hip-deep in mud and freezing cold in a dirt trench in the middle of Europe . . . It was 1918. His name was Jaynes, but almost no one called him that.

He was at that time in a man's life when he starts to wonder how in the heck he got in his predicament. He'd started out to be an engineer. He was going to college, doing fairly well in his studies, and really thought that engineering would be his lifework. Then World War I came along and things changed for him, as they did for most Americans. As he sat there so close to the front, something began to happen. He felt strange. Something new; something was not right. His eyes were burning, he couldn't breathe, and he had a deep painful clawing in his throat. Gas! Poison gas!

He had been warned about this, but he really didn't think it would happen. Poison gas might kill him, or make him go blind, or cause him to die a long painful death. He knew that our medics really didn't have a cure.

With all the strength that he could gather, he got out of that foxhole and ran. Covering his nose and mouth and gasping for air, he ran, desperately afraid to breathe the deadly air in his lungs. Oh, how his throat hurt. He did survive the horrible ordeal, although many in his platoon did not. And there seemed to be only one long-lasting effect. But it was something that everyone would notice every day for the rest of his life. His voice had changed. Something in the poison gas had damaged his vocal cords and now when he spoke, he just sounded funny.

He was embarrassed by his voice.

After the war he even left the country trying to find somewhere that people wouldn't laugh at him. Believe it or not, he tried growing pineapples in Guatemala for a while. But he hated that. People said that he sounded like an old codger. And I guess he did. Credit to the man, though—if you can't beat 'em, join 'em. If he was going to sound like an old codger . . . he'd find a way to make money at it. And he did. He made a lot of money at it.

It's a little-known fact that a poison gas attack gave Jaynes his career in show business. He made a lot of movies and even won three Oscars for his brillant portrayals of . . . an old codger. But I guess we'll always remember him best for his role as grandpa on the hit television show, *The Real McCoys*—the talented and funny-talking Walter Jaynes Brennan.

LITTLE-KNOWN FACT #50

The Assassin's Bullet

You might not know it, but it took a lot of guts to be president at the turn of the twentieth century. Just think back a minute . . . in 1865, Lincoln was shot and killed by an assassin. Just sixteen years later, President James Garfield also died from a bullet. And assassins had left a long trail of death in the twenty years since then. The president of France, czar of Russia, empress of Austria, shah of Persia, king of Italy . . . all were viciously murdered.

But in 1901, I guess you could say President William McKinley wasn't too awfully worried. "No one would want to hurt me," he assured his jumpy aides. McKinley was too busy cooking up a grand scheme to usher in the new century and celebrate his own reelection to worry about assassins. It was a time of big ideas . . . and his scheme had to be just as big. Remember, that was quite an era. Electric lights were starting to brighten up cities. People were talking to each other across long distances on new contraptions called telephones.

And McKinley had the distinction of being the first president to ride in a motorcar.

McKinley's staff threw a fit when he first unveiled his celebration plans: a cross-country train trip this country hasn't seen the likes of since. It would take him way out west and would conclude back in Buffalo, just in time for President's Day at the world-acclaimed Pan-American Exposition. That was where you could expect the new and the mind-boggling. People traveled from all over the world to see what great discoveries might change their lives in the twentieth century.

Though McKinley missed the President's Day speech, he finally made it to the exposition in early September. What he saw there fascinated him. He trudged tirelessly from building to building, shaking his head over the marvels that stood inside them.

McKinley's aides pleaded with him to go back to the White House and stay there. Investigations had uncovered six names on an anarchist's execution list. The first three were already dead, the fourth had survived countless attacks—and the fifth . . . well, that was hardheaded McKinley.

But on September 6, 1901, there stood McKinley in the Pan-American Temple of Music, eye to eye with his public. The Secret Service had a time of it. They were new on the job, really. Someone had the bright idea of assigning them to protect McKinley after they had outlived their usefulness as a spy ring.

And I guess you could say they botched their first job.

Agents failed to notice the killer standing in line . . . even though he held a gun covered with nothing but a handkerchief. When McKinley reached out to shake this man's hand, he was shot twice at point-blank range. The president and the assassin stood staring at each other, the crowd in shock. When Secret Service agents finally recovered enough to tackle the shooter, McKinley pleaded with them, "Don't hurt him, he's some poor misguided fellow."

Minutes later, McKinley was in the exposition's small emergency hospital. Doctors on call had no choice but to operate. They were frantic to recover the one bullet that was somewhere inside the president. They rigged up lights in the dim room and hoped for the best. But though they looked long and hard, doctors just couldn't find that bullet. All they could do was sew the president up and send him home.

Eight days after he was shot, William McKinley died. The bullet was still lodged somewhere in his back.

McKinley never lived long enough to enjoy the marvels of the twentieth century . . . and this is more true than you know. It's a little-known fact that just a few yards from where doctors operated on the president that fateful day there sat one of those marvelous new inventions, being shown for the first time—the X-ray machine. And one of the things it does best is find wayward bullets.

LITTLE-KNOWN FACT #51

Ben Franklin on the Case

There's no denying it, folks: Computers are here to stay. They are part of our everyday life now. As a matter of fact, we couldn't do this radio program without them.

And I have a feeling that as much as we like and enjoy the productivity that computers give us, there's nobody who would have loved to have had a computer more than Benjamin Franklin. You know, I believe that if he had been around fifty years ago, he probably would have invented the thing. But here's something that may surprise you.

There's something on your computer that Franklin did create, and something you use every day. I think old Ben would have loved e-mail, too. With just a few easy taps on a computer keyboard, we can talk to almost anyone anywhere, sending copies of messages, documents, memos, and so much more. Back in Ben's day, if you wanted to get a message to a bunch of folks, you had to print it—and that was not a quick or an easy thing to do.

If you go to Philadelphia, you can still see one of the original old wooden presses that Benjamin Franklin used to print his almanacs and other famous publications that made him the father of American inventions. Two strong men, working steadily at it, could turn out 180 sheets an hour. Does that sound like a lot? Well, it's not!

Today's offset presses can crank out over fifteen thousand sheets an hour. And back then, before you could print anything, you had to do a lot of hard work. It would take hours just to take the type out of the little drawers in the wooden cases and make words and sentences out of them. It took months just to learn how to do that.

And any of you young folks who are just starting a new job, consider this: A young man wanting to be a printer back in the colonial days would have to spend six years as an apprentice before he was considered skilled enough to do it on his own. After he would set the type, he would have to frame it and ink it. And that required some muscle, too, because they used leather-covered mallets called ink balls to pound the ink onto the plates. (And you thought it was hard to change the cartridge in your printer, right?) After the type was set, locked down, and inked, the printers would then pull a lever called a devil's tail to press the sheets of paper down onto the raised metal type. Try to imagine doing this in the summertime with no air-conditioning with the temperatures and the humidity hanging in the air at about ninety. Well, the hardware and working conditions may have changed, but some of the expressions are still with us . . . like that thing on your computer keyboard I mentioned that Ben Franklin came up with.

You see, back then, capital letters and small letters were kept in separate wooden cases stacked on top of each other to help the typesetter find them. And it's a little-known fact that when a printer two hundred years ago was setting type, he would take the capital letters from the "upper cases" above the printing press. The small letters were stored in—you got it—the lower cases.

LITTLE-KNOWN FACT #52

The Temperance Society

If you've heard much about Kansas, then you might know that it was a dry state a whole lot earlier and a whole lot longer than the rest of this country. When it was still just a territory, laws were so strict that liquor peddlers were made to feel mighty unwelcome. And when Kansas finally did become a state, Governor John P. St. John proposed early on that citizens "absolutely and forever" ban the sale of that "great evil" alcohol. Well, Kansans agreed with their sober leader, and in 1879 voted prohibition into their constitution.

Now, Harvey Wilcox was a Kansas man through and through . . . so when he and his wife retired and bought a beautiful, lush valley ranch somewhat west of Kansas, one of the first things they did was ban liquor on their property. Harvey was something of a self-made man, and he had made a fortune in real estate. So in no time at all, he'd divided that big ranch up . . . and before Harvey was done, he had an entire community mapped out.

But the rules were strict.

If you were going to live in Harvey's town, you had to swear off drinking, partying, and carrying on—just like they did in Kansas.

Up until the day he died, Harvey sold plots in his little temperance community. It was a quiet, blissful place to live. There was no crime to speak of . . . heck, nobody even owned a gun. And the last thing you had to worry about was somebody getting drunk and shooting up the place. Things were so peaceful, residents never bothered to lock up at night. In fact, there wasn't even a jail. And crowds, they were never a problem. The biggest headache the city council had was the farmers who kept driving their sheep through town square.

There was just one little problem. One widow found that she just couldn't bring in customers to her roadhouse inn without the promise of liquor. So when a group of travelers came around looking for a place to stay, she rented them her roadhouse, and then left town. She probably never even realized that she'd changed the future of that community forever. Come to find out, those travelers were a group called the Nestor Film Company. And it's a little-known fact that they established the first motion picture studio in a town that, eventually, would become full of them. You see, years ago, the Wilcoxes had named their little temperance society well. They called it Hollywood.

LITTLE-KNOWN FACT #53

A Case for Quilters

Some people think quilting is old-fashioned. Jan doesn't think so. She loves to quilt. She started quilting in 1991 and took to it like a duck to water. She's had several quilting classes and even taught some quilting herself. Jan is also a designer who's an expert at cutaway appliqué. She's so good at it, she's been on TV teaching her pattern making and demonstrating her fine appliqué work using freezer paper and needle-turning techniques.

You might say Jan started quilting and never looked back. She takes it with her everywhere—and I do mean everywhere. Why, you could see Jan with her cloth and needle and thread on an airplane, in a car, or at her hotel room—and you might think to yourself, "What a sweet old-fashioned girl." But this pretty blonde isn't as old-fashioned as her love for quilting might make her seem. Jan, you see, is a well-traveled woman.

But if you're a quilter and want to make one of Jan's favorite designs, you should be careful with your choice of colors. When she designed "Shooting Shuttles into Stars" for her Baltimore album quilt, she chose a light starry background fabric and a navy blue one for the four shuttles that make a circle on the block. Oh, you can go ahead and use those colors, but for the insignia design that is so delicately appliquéd between them, do not use a yellow or gold color fabric. You see, since your cloth hasn't been to space, you don't get to use gold.

It seems the astronauts are given a silver insignia pin when they're picked for a shuttle mission—and you can use a silver-gray color for yours. But when the astronauts get back from their first space flight, they get a gold insignia pin to wear to show that they've been in orbit around the earth in the space shuttle. And that gold color . . . it's very special. Only people or objects that have been in space get the privilege of wearing it.

Each astronaut gets to carry a few personal items in a really small bag on each mission, and Jan's quilting material got to fly into space. You might have a little more trouble getting your fabric into space than Jan did, though. How did Jan manage to use gold fabric for her quilts? Well, her fabric has flown on a shuttle mission. And she carried it!

You remember I told you Jan was well traveled, and she is . . . she's been around the world over four hundred times. It's a little-known fact that Jan Davis is one of NASA's space shuttle astronauts and one of America's foremost quilters!

LITTLE-KNOWN FACT #54

You Won't Believe Where We Got It

It has to be the most advanced form of travel yet devised, yet it has a two-thousand-year-old secret. I'm talking about the space shuttle. If you see it sitting on the launch pad, you can't help but notice those two massive solid rocket boosters attached to the sides of the main fuel tank. Those rockets help that big fella get into space. Couldn't do it without them! And as you know, they drop off a few minutes later when their fuel is spent and fall back into the sea.

You may not know that those big solid rocket boosters are made by a company called Thiokol at their factory in Utah. The engineers who designed those rockets may have preferred to make them a bit bigger or fatter, but they had a problem. The rockets had to get to the launch site to be attached to the shuttle, and there was only one way to get them there—the railroad. And the railroad line from the factory in Utah runs through a tunnel in the mountains. Those rockets had to fit through that tunnel.

Now, the U.S. standard railroad gauge or width is 4 feet, 8 1/2 inches. It's true, you can measure for yourself— just don't get hit by a train doing it. And the tunnel is only slightly wider than the rails.

You might be wondering how we got a 4-foot, 8 1/2-inch standard rail gauge. Well, it's because that's the way they built them in England, and the first U.S. railroads were built by English expatriates. And why did the English build them like that? Because the first rail lines were built by the same people who built the prerailroad tramways, and that's the gauge they used. Yeah, I know: Where did that come from?

Well, it seems that the folks who built the tramways used the same jigs and tools that they used for building wagons. Okay! Why did the wagons have that particular odd wheel spacing? Well, if they tried to use any other spacing, the wagon wheels would break on some of the old long-distance roads in England, because that's the spacing of the wheel ruts. So who built those old rutted roads? The first long-distance roads in Europe and England were built by imperial Rome for their legions. Those roads have been used ever since. And the ruts in the roads? They were formed by Roman war chariots, which everyone else had to match for fear of destroying their wagon wheels. Since the chariots were made by imperial Rome, they were all alike in the matter of wheel spacing. And imperial Roman war chariots were made just wide enough to accommodate the back ends of two war horses.

So U.S. standard railroad gauge of 4 feet, 8 1/2 inches derives from the original specification for an imperial Roman war chariot. Funny isn't it? . . . specifications and bureaucracies live forever, don't they!

And that brings us back to the original question of the rocket boosters fitting through the tunnel. The tunnel is slightly wider than the railroad track, and the railroad track is about as wide as two horses' behinds.

It's a little-known fact that the major design feature of what is arguably the world's most advanced transportation system—the space shuttle—was determined over two thousand years ago by the width of a horse's rear end!

LITTLE-KNOWN FACT #55

The Editor

Gail was twenty years old in 1821, and living in what was to become Jefferson County, Indiana. He worked as a teacher and was a respected and well-liked member of the community. Gail's only trouble was a bad cough that persisted throughout the Indiana winters. It was serious enough to make his doctor advise that Gail move away and seek a milder climate.

Gail followed his doctor's recommendation and moved to New Orleans. There, he heard that Texas was being opened to Americans for the first time . . . having previously been the exclusive domain of its Spanish rulers, Mexicans, and Indians. Gail was intrigued by the stories of enormous expanses of productive land and great herds of buffalo. While in New Orleans, Gail met Steve Austin, who would become the founder of Texas. Austin was looking for three hundred families to bring into the new territory—and Gail's would be one of them.

Gail got his land grant and began farming and raising cattle, but before long Austin asked for his help in mapping out the new territory, so Gail went to Austin's headquarters in San Felipe. When Austin went to Mexico City to petition for statehood, Gail was left in charge of the office.

When he returned, Austin told the colonists they were going to have to fight Santa Anna, the dictator behind the revolution in Mexico. Soon the battle began in Texas, and Gail again was left behind to run Austin's office . . . and, more importantly, to publish a newspaper that would rally support for the Texans' cause.

Gail worked hard. He collected every scrap of information about the enemy. He told readers of the bravery of Austin's troops, who had no training, no uniforms, and were badly outnumbered. He wrote about a small handful of men who held off Santa Anna's army for three weeks, only to be massacred in a mission near San Antonio. He printed the Texas Declaration of Independence on March

2, 1836 . . . and he headlined the battle cry of the new republic: "Remember the Alamo."

Still the Mexicans fought on. By the end of March, Texas seemed lost. Gail's paper spread the dire word and kept support and recruits coming. When Santa Anna arrived in San Felipe, Gail fled to Harrisburg with his equipment. He knew that the need for a newspaper to rally men behind the cause of freedom was never more urgent. Santa Anna came to Harrisburg in pursuit of Gail, who then escaped to Galveston. There the Mexicans succeeded in burning his print shop and dumping his press into the river.

A month later, the Texans captured Santa Anna . . . and Texas was preserved.

With the war over, Gail was delighted to have more time to devote to his rather peculiar hobby: food preservation. He brought big kettles into his barn. He made and stored row upon row of concentrated, canned food of all varieties: fruits, beef, chicken. He once threw a dinner party and served nothing but these concentrated foods to his puzzled guests.

Eventually he turned his attention to the preservation of one particular food, but he had a problem: when he used heat to concentrate it, it took on an unpleasant burned taste. Then he had the idea of using a vacuum pan instead, and the results were better. He knew he was on to something big. He could preserve indefinitely this food that usually spoiled within a few hours. Though people were skeptical at first, his new product grew to become highly prized—everyone who tasted it found they liked it. Soon demand outpaced production and Gail became famous.

Even today his name is recognized on supermarket

shelves everywhere . . . on cartons of milk, and bread, cheese, and ice cream. It's a little-known fact that the man who championed the still-famous battle cry "Remember the Alamo" later became dairyman to a nation: Gail Borden!

LITTLE-KNOWN FACT #56

The Man's Man

Teddy Roosevelt was our twenty-sixth president. I know I'm not really telling you anything you don't already know . . . but I might! Just wait a minute or so.

And although he became one of our most popular presidents, in the beginning a lot of folks feared that Teddy wasn't ready to be president. He ascended to office when William McKinley was assassinated. And at the time he was the youngest person ever to be president, only forty-two years old. Even before becoming president, though, he was popular.

I think it was because he was—well, a man's man! He was an athlete, an explorer, a cowboy, and a great environmentalist. He set aside millions of acres of land for future generations to enjoy, and he did this years before conservation was popular.

Did you know that he hated the name Teddy? But he knew it was great for publicity so he didn't say too much about it. He had served as a legislator and governor of New York State, and a police commissioner for New York City. But even when he was an assistant secretary of the navy, he longed for a more active life. And he got his wish when the Spanish-American War broke out.

Teddy resigned his administrative naval position and formed the first volunteer cavalry regiment. Teddy dubbed his regiment the "Rough Riders," and the Rough Riders were among the first American troops to fight the Spanish in Cuba. You probably remember reading about his heroic charge up San Juan Hill and victory. Or maybe you've seen one of movies that have been made about that historic event: horses at full gallop, swords drawn, men yelling as the Rough Riders charge up San Juan Hill. And it almost happened that way.

The Rough Riders had just landed at Daiquiri Beach, and Roosevelt set their sights on the vital position of San Juan Hill. And there is no question that Teddy and the Rough Riders showed great courage and cunning as he led his Rough Riders charging up the hill to defeat the enemy. The rush of the gallant horsemen up the hill quickly became legendary. Soon, boys all over the country were reenacting Teddy's great cavalry charge up San Juan Hill.

And as I said, it almost happened that way . . . .but not quite. You see, when the Rough Riders landed, San Juan Hill was very well defended by the Spanish and could have easily fended off a cavalry charge. Roosevelt was brave, but not stupid. He noticed, however, that right next to San Juan Hill was another hill that was lightly defended. Once they secured this, they were able to fire at the Spanish forces on San Juan Hill, forcing them to abandon their position.

It's a little-known fact that Teddy Roosevelt and the Rough Riders never did charge up San Juan Hill. No, he charged up Kettle Hill. Teddy did ride up San Juan Hill, all right, but only after the enemy had fled. Later Roosevelt remarked that taking San Juan Hill was one of the most satisfying days of his life—satisfying because he was able to use tactics and strategy to save lives.

LITTLE-KNOWN FACT #57

One Tough Hombre

He was determined to make a fresh start. He was in a new town, had a new wife, and even decided to use his middle name so no one would know him. And San Diego was the place to be. A boomtown!

Berry had decided it would be the perfect place for he and his new bride Josephine to build a life together. It had taken him a lot of years to find the woman he wanted to spend his life with, and he wanted to impress her. Berry didn't have much money, just a little he'd saved here and there over time. But he made it go a long way. He had a few investments, got into real estate. Then, as the town grew . . . well, so did Berry and Josephine's fortunes.

Before long he bought a saloon, then another. A couple of hotels came after that. Within a few months he owned pretty much the entire "gas-lamp quarter" of old San Diego. Josephine was sure proud of him. Proud of the life they were making together.

But you know how boomtowns are . . . something always happens to stir things up and ruin a good thing. Now that Berry had things just about the way he wanted them, along came some Jake Leg, who wanted in on the action. Berry had worked hard to build his business, and he didn't take too kindly to this Johnny-come-lately. This fella opened a saloon right across the street from Berry's.

The fella later said that he probably wouldn't have done it if he had known who Berry was. Well, Berry convinced his distributors not to supply his competitor. He explained things to them so they understood that he would be very unhappy if they did. He pretty much told his staff the same thing . . . especially his showgirls.

You might guess that the new competitor across the street wasn't about to give up that easily. And the fellow hired a few tough guys to protect the place. I might mention about now that Berry was one hombre who was used to getting his way. So he hired a few tough guys to break a few windows across the street, knock about the bartenders a little bit, and generally make a mess of things. Berry's competitor finally got the message, and he bailed out of the saloon business.

And wouldn't you know it—after all that, Berry got cabin fever. He heard about the gold strike in Alaska, and that sounded more like where he wanted to be. Josephine went right along with him. So Berry sold out—and he sold everything to the same man who'd tried to horn in on him a year or so before. The man was a bit surprised after everything that had happened. But not nearly as surprised as he was when he found out who Berry really was.

It's a little-known fact that one of San Diego's toughest businessmen, in the years after Dodge City and Tombstone, was Marshal Wyatt Berry Earp.

LITTLE-KNOWN FACT #58

Daughter Knows Best?

All Sarah knew was that she was in love. Like most young women her age, she had dreamed that her knight in shining armor would ride up and rescue her, but there was a problem. Oh, she had found her knight all right! His name was Jeff. And Sarah loved him. Jeff loved her. They wanted to be married. Jeff had even done the right thing and asked her father for her hand in marriage.

And that took a lot of courage . . . you see, Sarah's daddy was Zachary Taylor! That's right, the man who would become president. Even now he was a general in the army and on the fast track to the White House. Jeff was a lieutenant in her daddy's command. It should have been a sure thing. But her father had said no. And that was a problem. You see, General Taylor led American forces against Mexico during the Mexican-American War.

One of the officers under his command was Jeff, and Taylor didn't think much of Jeff as a solider and an officer. Evidently that was enough to stop a wedding. But you know what? Headstrong Sarah did it anyway.

That's right, Sarah defied her father and married Jeff, becoming estranged from her family in the process.

Now, I know you want me to say that love will conquer all and that Sarah and Jeff lived happily ever after. But they didn't! As a matter of fact, the beautiful young Sarah, who had turned her back on her father and her entire family . . . died of malaria only three months after the wedding. But believe it or not, that wasn't the end of Zachary

Taylor and the young Jeff's relationship. At the Battle of Monterey, Taylor saw Jeff in battle, leading a regiment of volunteers. Jeff fought intelligently and valiantly. General Taylor realized what a fine leader Jeff was.

You see, the victory at Monterey turned Zach Taylor into a highly touted presidential candidate. And he owed much of his popularity to Jeff. A few months later, young Jeff was badly wounded in the Battle of Buena Vista. General Zachary Taylor personally saw to his care. As Jeff recuperated from his wounds, the soon-to-be-president was heard to say, "My daughter was a better judge of men than I."

After the war, Taylor became president, and the two men became even closer friends. The two families often celebrated holidays together, and Jeff was a frequent visitor to the White House. Well, it's a little-known fact that years earlier, Zachary Taylor had forbidden his daughter from marrying the man of her dreams . . . but she did it anyway. And who knows what might have happened if Taylor had given his daughter permission to marry . . . the next president.

Yes, I said president!

Not of the United States, but of the Confederacy. You see, Sarah became Mrs. Jefferson Davis.

LITTLE-KNOWN FACT #59

Firewood for Your Car?

A lot of us complain about the price of gas these days, and probably rightfully so, since it just seems to be going up and up. Still, there have been times when gasoline wasn't just expensive, but also in very short supply. This is especially true in wartime, when gasoline supplies are needed for the vehicles and equipment used in fighting.

That's exactly the situation that the French found themselves in during World War II. They had a problem finding gas to run their cars. Much of the reason was us. Between the Americans and the Brits, you see, we controlled much of the seas. So, the French looked about for alternatives. Amazing as it may sound to us now, around about 1942, if you looked in a Frenchman's gas tank, well, you wouldn't find one!

But you might find a stack of firewood in the trunk. Or a jug of cooking oil.

Now, how could you run a car on firewood or cooking oil? Well, Emile Gagnan, a French Canadian engineer who worked for Air Liquid France, was well known for inventions. His gadgets were widely used in the French air force. Since gasoline was in short supply, Emile set about to figure out a way to keep cars running on whatever fuel their drivers could find. Well, anyone knows that if you just pour cooking oil or firewood in a car's fuel tank, you're not going to go anywhere, but Emile hit on an ingenious device.

You see, the firewood would burn as a charcoal gas, and then it went through a regulator to the engine. Believe it or not, it worked. After that, French folks started driving around with their trunks full of firewood or cooking oil.

But then a couple of things happened in the war that led Emile to work out a new use for his device. You see, by now the Allies were getting a leg up on the Germans. They had run them out of Italy, and America and Britain controlled most of the shipping lanes by now. So the Germans were running out of gas supplies. The German high command got wind of these French cars running off burning wood and cooking oil, so they went to the French and demanded that they come up with an alternative fuel for their war machines. The French navy came to Air Liquid France, and Air Liquid sent them our man Emile Gagnan. Emile went to work on a device and he recruited his friend Jacques to test the apparatus. Some friend Emile was— Jacques almost got killed several times in the process.

But between them, they developed a workable regulator for compressed air. By the time the two men perfected it, however, the war was nearly over and the Germans had little use for the funny little invention. But Emile and Jacques did!

It's a little-known fact that the first fully workable self-contained compressed air regular, which was invented to fuel automobiles with firewood during World War II . . . became scuba apparatus for underwater diving. And even though the device was never effectively used by the Germans, it opened a whole new area of underwater exploration for humankind—and a fabulous new career, and legend, for the man who was nearly killed several times in developing it. And that, of course, was Emile's friend and guinea pig diver—Jacques. Jacques Yves Cousteau!

LITTLE-KNOWN FACT #60

Senta Makes His Mark

His name was Senta. And he lived quite a long time ago. We're not sure exactly when, but we do know that it was in the region that we now call Mexico.

Senta was something special to the people of his little hamlet because he was their silent and secretive protector. Not from the authorities or some conquering army as is so often the case. No, Senta protected his people from José de la Garcia, the reigning monarch in the territory! You see, Senta's whole family and all of his friends worked on Garcia's ranches and farms. The work was hard, sunup to sundown, seven days a week.

By all accounts, Garcia was a harsh and unforgiving master who drove humans like he drove horses. And he was the absolute authority in the land. Many of Senta's family were either slaves or conscript labor. They were bound to Garcia and couldn't leave even if they wanted to. No matter how harsh the treatment, no mater how long the hours, no matter how poor the living conditions, they couldn't leave! To make sure, Garcia had a small band of vicious outlaws who acted like an army. They protected Garcia from invaders, and tracked down and either beat or killed any worker trying to escape. Beatings were common. Food scarce. Money for the workers nonexistent. That's where Senta came in.

After seeing the way that Garcia treated his people, Senta would often sneak into El Patron's compound and steal food, money, and even jewelry. He didn't keep the things, he gave them to the workers so that they could trade for other needed items, like medicines and material and weapons. All this of course to the enormous frustration of the cruel Garcia.

Garcia put a price on Senta's head. But it was never collected. No one would reveal the whereabouts of the elusive Senta. Garcia died at a fairly early age, and we don't know exactly what happened to Senta after that. And you may be asking why I'm even telling you all this. Well, does any of this sound familar?

It did to Johnston McCulley, a reporter for the *Police Gazette* in 1919. Johnston was something of a history buff and often spent time running down stories like this one, just for fun. It's a little-known fact that Johnston McCulley wrote "The Curse of Capistrano" right after reading about Senta. And the "curse of Capistrano" first introduced us to McCulley's fertile imagination and his creation: Zorro!

LITTLE-KNOWN FACT #61

In the Palm of His Hand

It just wasn't going right. And it was so important that this did go just right. Vina was trying, but it just wasn't coming out the way it should. The director came over and asked Vina what the problem was. After all, she was a seasoned actress and had done dozens of scenes before a camera.

Vina said she wasn't sure . . . but she was. She was supposed to lie on the special prop that had been built for this scene and scream. She knew how to scream all right, but when the time came, she just couldn't. She would lie back and start crying. The director and the crew were baffled. Why was she crying?

Well, the reason was very personal. It all started for Vina when she was just four years old back in Canada. One very cold and blustery day in the midst of the Canadian winter, Vina was being pulled across a lake on her sled by her eleven-year-old brother and his friend. The trio was about halfway across the lake when they hit a crack in the ice. Suddenly Vina's brother was in the water over his head and Vina and the sled were sliding in right behind him. The water was freezing cold and Vina didn't know how to swim. Her brave young brother seemed to sense what to do, though. He righted himself and lifted Vina out of the water. Vina struggled to get back on the ice and solid footing, but she kept slipping back in the freezing lake. Finally her brother simply held her up out of the water in safety, until his friend ran for help. Rescue came in time for Vina, but not her brother. He died saving his little sister.

And now, twenty years later, in the middle of this movie set, every time Vina laid her head back and got into the position that the scene required . . . she remembered that day and her brother. And the tears flowed.

It's a little-known fact that it took a very long time to get that scene right, but they did, and it became one of the biggest movies of its time. Still revered today as a marvel of special effects and moviemaking. And one young actress had to overcome her past and her memories to get it right . . . every time Vina Fay Wray lay back on the giant hand of King Kong!

LITTLE-KNOWN FACT #62

The Ordinary Seaman

Sam really didn't like being on shipboard that much, but here he was. When it was all said and done, he really didn't have much choice. To say that Sam had a difficult childhood would be an understatement—what with his mother dying when he was young and his sister committing suicide. At one time his family had been well off, but by the time Sam was fourteen, all the family's resources had been squandered. To make matters worse, Sam was a terrible student. His father told him he should go off and be a sailor.

So here he was.

The ship was the *Carvo*, which was set to sail around the world, probably for the China trade. Now, Sam knew that men made fortunes in the China trade, but not if they were ordinary seamen. And in 1830, it took nearly a year to make a round trip. As a seaman he worked hard. Life on ship consisted of long hours of work and long hours of boredom. If he wasn't on his watch, there was nothing to do. Most of the men had some little hobby of some kind to occupy their time. Those who could, read. But most couldn't. Sam, he whittled. A little skill he picked up from the ship's carpenter. In fact, the capstan, that big wooden cylinder with the sprocket rods coming out of it that is used to pull up the anchor, caught his attention and gave him an idea. One that would change life almost every-where in the world, and certainly a long way from the ocean where he got it.

And he spent a good part of his year carving a model of his idea.

But he didn't come away from his year as a seaman with much more than that. Once back on land, he con-vinced John Pearson to make a prototype. And it took Pearson two years to do so. Finally the working copy was done . . . and Sam applied and received a patent. Within a few years, Sam's invention was hailed as the most signifi-cant single item in the West.

Actually, it tamed the West.

Soon, people everywhere were saying: "God didn't cre-ate all men equal . . . Sam did!" It's a little-known fact that the capstan of a sailing ship was the inspiration for Sam's invention: a revolving chamber in a gun. Sam Colt's Colt 45!

LITTLE-KNOWN FACT #63

The Disaster Movie

The huge luxury ship set sail, and the passengers were ready to enjoy a wonderful cruise. This would be more than just a vacation—it was going to be the cruise of a lifetime. The staterooms were magnificent. The food was exceptional. The entertainment was first-rate. The crew members were determined to give the passengers the best service possible, and the facilities were extravagant.

There were the usual exercise and entertainment offerings, such as movie theaters and stages for musical revues.

Then a few days out to sea, things started to go wrong. The ship started sinking and passengers were trapped below decks in a fight for their life. Some made it, but most did not. Do you remember *The Poseidon Adventure*? The movie about the sinking of a luxury liner?

You probably do . . . it was a huge hit in the 1970s. But you may not be aware that there is more than one version of that movie. In both versions, however, the ship turns upside down, and the passengers who survive the initial catastrophe have to make it to the upturned bottom of the boat to get to safety.

You know, most folks know that for the most part, it's just a flat bad idea to show a movie about an airline disaster to people sitting on an airplane. Makes them kind of jumpy. Some folks are pretty skittish about flying to begin with, much less someone priming the pump with a crashed-airplane movie.

And the same is true of ships. It's just not cricket to show a movie about folks drowning to people way out in the middle of the ocean. But that's just what the entertainment director on this cruise did, all right! I'm not kidding. Down on deck two in the ship's movie theater they were showing the film *The Poseidon Adventure*. Funny thing was, the passengers loved the movie. They found the depiction of the disaster convincing, too—and this was a tough crowd to please, since they were, after all, on a ship themselves!

And wouldn't you know it, halfway through the movie one night . . . their own ship began to sink! Let me tell you, folks, you couldn't write a script like this one. But it's true! Just like in the movie, there weren't enough lifeboats, and the captain tried his best to cope with the disaster as the crew helped women and children into the few lifeboats. Over fiteen hundred people died in a gruesome enactment of the movie many of them had been watching.

Now, you'll remember that I told you there was more than one version of *The Poseidon Adventure*. And the one being shown on this ill-fated cruise was a brand-new movie from esteemed director D. W. Griffith. Well, it's a little-known fact that the original version of *The Poseidon Adventure* has been mostly forgotten, perhaps because one of its first showings was on board . . . the *Titanic*!

LITTLE-KNOWN FACT #64

The British Invasion

Well, folks, it was the shot heard 'round the island. The island of San Juan, that is, just off the Washington coast, west of Seattle. This was back in the summer of 1859.

An American farmer by the name of Lyman Cutler had had enough. When he walked out on his porch that June morning, he had no idea that his actions would bring America and Britain musket to musket one more time. But a man has to defend his property.

His property was being invaded—again. This was not the first time. He had put up with this violation of his land just one time too many and, as they say these days, he was not going to take it anymore.

He took careful aim with his trusty rifle and fired. The invader fell dead. Lyman had hoped it wouldn't come to this but now that it had, he was glad it was over. And his property was his once again.

Well, that wasn't the end of it. Not too many hours had passed before the British authorities on San Juan Island had heard about the shooting and announced that they were going to arrest Lyman Cutler and take him over to the mainland, to British Columbia, for a proper trial. Well, as you might imagine, the Americans on the island would hear none of it. They told Lyman to just stay put.

Well, friends, this argument smoldered for weeks. Finally, when the British authorities got just a little too insistent, the Americans called in the military.

Captain George Pickett arrived with troops and immediately proclaimed San Juan to be American territory. They were there to protect Lyman Cutler, he declared.

Naturally, the British did not agree. The very next week, sixty-one Royal Marines arrived on the island to claim it for Britain.

You know how they say the courts move slow these days? Well, we don't have anything on these folks. I'm not kidding when I tell you that it took twelve years for this dispute to be resolved. Yep, for twelve years the British had warships in San Juan Harbor pointed at the American soldiers who had their muskets ready and were not about to give up the island.

It is a little-known fact that America and Britain almost went to war—for the third time—and probably would have, except for the Civil War. And all because Lyman Cutler had walked out on his porch in June 1859 and shot dead the intruder in his vegetable garden: one fat black British pig.

LITTLE-KNOWN FACT #65

The Stricken Soldier

The year was 1862. Our country was engaged in a bloody Civil War between the North and the South . . . the Union and the Confederacy. It was a very sad time in our country's history, and it would get worse before it got better.

As the story goes, a Union army captain—Robert Elli-combe—was with his men near Harrison's Landing in Virginia. The Confederate army was on the other side of the narrow strip of land. The two sides had fought earlier that day, to no avail. And they were still shooting back and forth, even in the dark.

Late that night, Captain Ellicombe heard the moan of a soldier who lay mortally wounded on the field. Not knowing if it was a Union or Confederate soldier, the captain decided to risk his life and bring the stricken man back for medical attention. It was so dark on that battlefield, the captain had to navigate by the sounds of the moaning soldier; he couldn't see a thing. Crawling on his stomach through the gunfire, he reached the stricken soldier and began pulling him toward his encampment.

It was when the captain finally reached his own lines that he discovered it was actually a Confederate soldier, and the captain was too late . . . the soldier was dead. The captain lit a lantern. Suddenly, he caught his breath and went numb with shock. In the dim light, he saw the face of the soldier. It was his own son. The boy had been studying music in the South when the war broke out. Without telling his father, he enlisted in the Confederate army.

The following morning, heartbroken, the father asked permission of his superiors to give his son a full military burial despite his enemy status. His request was only partially granted. The captain had asked if he could have a group of army band members play a funeral dirge for the son at the funeral. That request was turned down since the soldier was a Confederate.

But out of respect for the father, they did give him one musician. The captain chose a bugler. He asked the bugler to play a series of musical notes he had found on a piece of paper in the pocket of his dead son's uniform. This wish was granted.

This music was the haunting melody we now know as "Taps," which is used at all military funerals—evidently written by the very man at whose funeral it was played for the first time.

LITTLE-KNOWN FACT #66

The Warmhearted Southern Belle

Can you imagine how Mary Anderson felt? Here she was, a proper southern lady who had come up all the way from Alabama to New York City. It was cold, oh, so cold in New York in the winter of 1903. Mary had come up to see the big city as a tourist. Of course, at that time cameras were about the size of a table, and folks weren't prone to carrying them around.

So Mary brought her sketchpad.

She was going to do a little sketching of the tall buildings and then show them to her friends back home and tell them about the big city way up north. Those buildings must have seemed magnificent to a lady who had come all the way from Alabama; Mary must have had a busy pencil. She just had the ambition to go anywhere and everywhere. But she hadn't counted on those cold northern winters.

In Alabama—well, they had a little winter, but nothing like what she faced in New York City. I mean, snow was something she'd read about, but that didn't tell you how cold your fingers got, or how your nose would run . . . or your feet . . . oh, her feet were cold. And unlike Alabama, the cold didn't go away. It lasted months. Her friends had told her that the best way to get around the big city was by the streetcars. So Mary Anderson went by streetcar and she wrote in her journal that she was most admiring of the streetcar drivers—how skilled, kind, and courteous they were to a lady.

Mary was a tender-hearted soul who didn't like to see people having a hard time. So she became upset for the streetcar drivers when she saw them having such a terrible time with the snow and ice. You see, they were constantly having to stop the streetcar, get out, run up front, and make adjustments. When they came back into the warm car, why, Mary could see that their hands were nearly frozen blue each time.

Then Mary had an idea. She whipped out her sketchpad and started drawing a device she figured would help those poor motormen. It would let them drive the streetcars without ever having to get out because of bad weather. She sketched a spring-loaded swinging arm with a rubber blade on the outside of the windshield that could be moved back and forth by a hand lever inside the cab. Her friends teased her about it, but Mary was determined to patent her invention, which she did in 1904.

It's a little-known fact that Mary Anderson, a southern belle who felt sorry for some cold but kindly street car drivers . . . invented the windshield wiper. And by 1913 her little sympathetic invention had become standard equipment on every automobile made.

LITTLE-KNOWN FACT #67

The Incredible, Edible . . . Car?

You know, I've heard them called geniuses and some of them may be. But I'm here to tell you that not everything these geniuses do is genius material! Oh, we've all heard of the captains of industry and some of them might come close to deserving the title. But not always.

And it's funny how we almost never hear about those times. We remember how a very smart fellow named Lee Iacocca came along just at the right time, with the right amount of smarts, industry knowledge, and clout to save an entire car company from bankruptcy. He even took that broke company and elevated it to number one in the industry.

And we've so often heard of Thomas Edison and his electric lightbulb and phonograph player . . . but did you ever hear about his sound muffling device? It made so much noise that you couldn't hear what you were trying to drown out. Kind of a bad idea.

Or take Alexander Graham Bell. We owe him the telephone all right, but we also owe him the bread flattener. Yep, something he invented to make bread flatter. I don't know why he thought it needed to be flatter, and evidently no one else thought so either, because it didn't work out very well. Or how about that fella who wanted to build an all-edible soybean car? That's right, he conceived of an all-natural car. I guess you could eat if you ever got hungry. He was something of a health food nut to begin with. He ate only natural foods and shied away from a lot of the conventional medicines and cures of the day in favor of what he perceived to be the natural way of health. He often took his message on the road with him when he traveled and almost never failed to promote what he considered to be the benefits of eating and living naturally.

And he probably went farther than anyone else would have with what most would consider an bad idea—this edible car thing. He actually went out and bought up some farms and started raising soybeans. He contracted with other soybean farmers to sell him all their crops. He even went so far as to build several soybean processing plants in order to make the soybeans into a shape and consistency that would hold up under the rigors of driving on the open roads. Well, it didn't work out . . . you've never seen a soybean car, have you? And can you imagine what an automotive genius like Henry Ford would have thought about this idea of a soybean car? A man who obviously knew what it took to make an automobile? Well, you don't have to wonder. It's a little-known fact that the man who spent millions to develop the first edible soybean car was, in fact, Henry Ford.

LITTLE-KNOWN FACT #68

The "Poet of Bran"

During the early years of the nineteenth century, New England saw its share of religious diversity. The new American nation, after all, had been founded on religious freedom, and nowhere was that more evident than in the Northeast.

There were the traditional Anglicans, Presbyterians, and Congregationalists, whose roots lay in England. But the voices of American Baptists and Methodists were also beginning to be heard in chorus with modern American perspectives, like Emerson and Thoreau. The old Puritan New England was fading. Americans had come full circle.

And the principle of religious freedom was being put into practice in many forms, from the traditional to the bizarre. Americans had an overwhelming sense that God was on their side. In fact, when founding fathers Thomas Jefferson and John Adams both died on the Fourth of July, 1826, it was seen by many to be a sign of God's blessing on the plan for American liberty.

Now, this new religious freedom spawned its share of eccentrics. Unusual religious leaders began to put in an appearance in many places. One of the more colorful figures in this spectrum of faith was a Presbyterian minister from Connecticut named Sylvester, a minister who was destined to make an impact on America far greater than even he could have imagined.

Sylvester was a sickly fellow. All his life he'd suffered from various and persistent ailments. In fact, he'd even gone so far as to marry his nurse so that he would have full-time professional care. By the time he was ordained, he'd become a self-styled physician, using the expertise that he thought he'd gained fighting his own illnesses to help others in need of a sound body as well as a sound soul.

By the late 1820s, Sylvester had become a well-known figure on the New England scene, touring the area to deliver his lectures on the benefits of his special program of purity.

He preached a strict doctrine of abstinence, temperance, and purity in all things. His followers refused all meat and most oils. Drank nothing but water. Bathed very frequently. And slept with the windows open even at the height of the New England winter. All in the service of saving their souls.

As his popularity grew, the reverend began to make more and more specific recommendations about the lifestyle that would put his followers on the path to righteousness. In 1837, he published a book recommending that those who sought the kingdom of heaven should for-sake all baked goods not made in the home. He claimed that the flour processing that went on in commercial bak-eries diminished the purity of the goods they sold and cor-rupted the original, God-given form of the grain. He became so committed to this viewpoint that his neigh-bor—Ralph Waldo Emerson—came to call him the "poet of bran."

Naturally, local bakers did not take kindly to this phi-losophy. It is a mark of Sylvester's influence that New England bakers felt the need to picket and harass him whenever he appeared in public!

Unfortunately, these dietary restrictions did the rev-erend little good, and he died at age fifty-seven, sickly to the end. His preaching, however, lived on. For had it not been for this slightly and sickly man, you might not have had your breakfast today!

You see, his name became associated with a certain type of natural, unprocessed flour that is enjoyed to this very day, in breakfast cereals, kids' cookies, and even piecrusts. It's a little-known fact that the preacher who taught his followers not to eat meat and processed flour would have his namesake served up on treats called S'mores—the Reverend Sylvester Graham.

LITTLE-KNOWN FACT #69

Nation-Building Is Tough

I've never met King Robert the First, but I'd like to. I know it's probably not easy being king of anywhere, but if you were the reigning monarch of the postage stamp–sized country of Talossa, well, you'd have your share of problems. Talossa's what you might call a micronation, one of the smallest on the face of the earth. Now add that to the fact that Talossa has no army, a tiny economy, and is surrounded on three sides by a major world power . . . and you probably see why King Robert might worry. To hear him tell it, his powerful neighbor hasn't been too forthright about the plight of Talossa. The best he can say is that it hasn't, as of right now, refuted Talossa's right to exist.

I've already said Talossa is no giant place. But it does have a couple of other claims to land. Talossa annexed a chunk of Antarctica a few years back: Pengopats—that's what they call it—has never been colonized by any other nation.

Talossa also makes claim to a small island off the coast of Brittany; in 1982, it became a province. But not without a struggle. Too small really to call it a war. In 1984, French troops occupied a portion of the island and placed it behind barbed wire. King Robert and the prime minister of Talossa eventually sailed out to their province and liberated a portion of the French occupied zone. Of course they had to go themselves, seeing as how Talossa has no army. The pair would have liked to have liberated the entire area, but the barbed wire was loose in only one place. So with few tools and only two men, they did what they could. And went on a picnic to celebrate afterward.

The population of Talossa is still pretty small today. At last count only about sixty people claimed Talossan citizenship and only a third of those actually live in the country itself. One of the hot issues in the legislature is the problem of inactive citizens. Only about 58 percent voted in the last election. Also, Talossans wonder about immigration. How fast should Talossa be growing? And debate continues in the hallowed halls of the legislature, where the progressive conservative party still has the majority, over a recent historical work that suggests Talossans are direct descendants of the mysterious Berbers. Argument has been hot and heavy over that one.

Existence for the Talossans is day to day. But King Robert plans to enjoy his country's freedom and independence while he can. Even though Talossans say it's obvious that the powerful government to the east, west, and south has no complaints, since it's never bothered to dispute Talossa's claims to nationhood. It's still a shaky existence at best, because it's a little-known fact that the kingdom of Talossa originated when thirteen-year-old Robert Madison declared his bedroom a sovereign, independent nation in 1979. And Talossa has grown steadily since.

But the only problem is, it's grown to cover thirteen square kilometers of land that the United States of America might take issue with . . . since it sits, after all, right smack dab in the middle of Milwaukee.

LITTLE-KNOWN FACT #70

Look Away . . .

Well, neighbors, if you like poetry, I guess you like that famous poem by Henry Wadsworth Longfellow: "*Evangeline.*" It's a beautiful story about the French people in Nova Scotia, which used to be called Acadia. When the British took over up there, the French people were thrown out of that country, and about three thousand of them found their way to Louisiana. Down there, they were still known as Acadians. Say that three times fast—*acadian, acadjun, acajun*—you can see where the word *Cajun* came from. Now, remember that, because it's gonna take us where we're going in this story with a surprising little twist at the end.

Naturally, these folks brought their wonderful French culture with them when they came to the new land. It still is quite prevalent in the food, in the music, and in the ways of the people.

This was a boom time for that part of America. Thousands of people were migrating down there to get in on the excitement and the adventure of the new cities strung along the Mississippi River.

There was a lot of money to be made by smart, quick businessmen in those days. Quite a few of them turned out to Acadians, who began to influence the society in Louisiana and for miles around.

Why, a lot of the commerce in that part of America was being done in French. Many of the boat captains did all their financial dealings in French banknotes.

Just like a dollar bill is today, the most common banknote in those days was the ten-dollar note. Now, because it was printed in French, it naturally had the word for "ten" on it. In French, that's pronounced *dee*—but it's spelled d-i-x.

Problem was, a lot of visitors from the other states did not speak French. So when they got hold of one of these ten-dollar notes, they pronounced it with the x. It's a little-known fact that it was the Cajuns who gave the southern states their most popular nickname when English-speaking visitors started calling the place where a French ten-dollar bill came from: "Dix-ie."

LITTLE-KNOWN FACT #71

The Competition

Jim was born in the tiny little village of Callan in County Kilkenny, Ireland. One thing that became very evident, even at a young age, was that Jim could draw and draw very well indeed.

Jim was raised on a farm and, like most of the young men in Ireland in those days, he enjoyed the good times. The terrible famines that would wipe out 50 percent of the potato crop were still a hundred years away. So it wasn't a tragedy that brought young James Hoban to America. No, it was the thrill of adventure and his desire to see this new land and try to make a living for himself with this skill he had with pen and ink. You see, Jim had become a fine architect.

Jim had eagerly read the reports on the Revolutionary War going on over in this country and he knew it was his destiny, so he left his home in Ireland and set out for the new nation across the ocean. But as fate would have it, the war ended before he landed in America.

His first stop in the New World was Philadelphia. But soon Jim made his way down to Charleston in South Carolina. Here there was work for a budding architect— especially one who could combine European influences with an eye for the innovative designs that were becoming popular in the new country.

Jim set out to show Charleston what he could do. It wasn't long before he became fairly busy and his wonderful new designs were attracting the attention of builders and designers alike. He became sought after for his creative concepts—a number of Charleston homes still show the mark of this Irishman who had become American. Then came word of a competition, a great chance for an architect—and there was a substantial prize of five hundred dollars for the best designs.

And folks, back in those days, that was a lot of money.

What's more, Jim knew that another man—something of a famous and revered gentleman from Virginia—was also entering the contest. Jim knew that the competition would be fierce . . . so he turned in what he considered to be his best work. His concept was bold: a neoclassical look that he had admired so much as a boy in Ireland. He gave it his very best effort, all right. Then there was nothing to do but wait. Finally, after weeks and weeks of suspense, the announcement was made: Jim had won the competition.

It is a little-known fact that James Hoban—an Irish immigrant—won the competition to design, believe it or not, the White House. And that other architect . . . the one whom Jim beat out for the rights to design our president's house? Well, that would be a fellow who would later occupy the very house that Jim designed: Thomas Jefferson.

LITTLE-KNOWN FACT #72

The World's Most Famous Waffle

Bill was not the kind of guy who usually wasted time daydreaming at the breakfast table. Everybody at college knew that! He was a dedicated, hardworking member of the faculty. He was the track coach and a no-nonsense kind of a guy. So it was unusual, to say the least, for Bill to just sit and stare. But this morning was different. Bill just stared at his breakfast waffle. There was something about the pattern that fascinated him. All those little squares. That repetition of little squares. He knew there was something in that pattern that was trying to tell him something.

The first thing Bill did was to call his partner, Phil, and tell him that he had an idea. The two men had been best friends for quite a while—which is why they had teamed up and started a company together. And their company was actually doing okay. Sales were good and their product was top quality. But Bill knew they could improve on it, and he was pretty sure he had just seen the solution in his breakfast waffle. Now, whenever Bill got that look in his eye, his wife braced herself. She knew that when he got one of his ideas, he became so determined and focused on finding the solution that she knew the best thing she could do was just stand back and get the heck out of his way. But she suspected by the way he was staring at that waffle it was going to cost her another one of her favorite kitchen appliances.

And sure enough . . . well, she might as well say goodbye to her favorite waffle iron right now!

Because the next thing that happened is that Bill took her waffle iron out into the garage and proceeded to destroy it. How did he do that? By pouring chemicals onto the waffle iron. He knew that he was close to something big, so he poured all kinds of strange combinations of chemicals onto his wife's waffle iron and then would take the finished product outside and test it. And it's a good thing he did; after all, the first time he tested his creation, it crumbled into a hundred pieces.

But finally, Bill hit paydirt. After dozens of different

combinations, he finally mixed up some latex with a few other chemicals and came up with just what he was looking for. And a billion-dollar business was born.

You remember Bill was the track coach at the University of Oregon? Well, what he was looking for with that waffle iron was a better track shoe. It's a little-known fact that the material that he cooked up on his wife's waffle iron turned out to be the sole for the long-distance running shoe that he and his buddy Phil Knight started putting in the shoes they sold in their new company—one they named Nike.

LITTLE-KNOWN FACT #73

For The Love of a Pin Cushion

It was one of the most successful contest promotions they had ever had. The Gold Medal flour company was always looking for ways to promote their product, and this looked like a good way to do it.

What they did was come up with an idea for a puzzle. They told customers that if they could solve this little puzzle, why, they would send them a pincushion. Can you imagine a quiz show today called "Who Wants to Win a Pincushion"?

This was back in 1921, though, and apparently pincushions were mighty popular, because the company got thousands of entries in this little puzzle contest—and most of 'em were right.

Well, now Gold Medal had to make good on the contest, so they ordered up thousands of pincushions and got to work on a letter that would go out with the little prize. You see, there were a lot of dedicated customers, and the Gold Medal flour company wanted to keep 'em around, buying up that flour.

So they composed a very friendly letter, thanking the ladies—it was mostly ladies who'd won the pincushions—and telling them that the company hoped they enjoyed using their pincushions. And, of course, they would be most grateful if the ladies would purchase Gold Medal flour the next time they were planning on doing some baking.

Well, all the big shots at Gold Medal agreed it was a right nice letter, but they felt it really ought to come from a person, not from some big corporation. So they thought about it and after a while, they decided to use Bill's name. Bill was one of the directors of the company and he had a real friendly-sounding name.

The only thing was, a lot of the women who worked at the Gold Medal flour company thought the letter really ought to come from a woman. It would be okay if they used Bill's last name, but why not make up a woman's name to go along with it? So they held a little contest in the company to come up with a lady's name. And they ended up sending out thousands of letters signed by a name that would become one of the top brand names in the country.

It's a little-known fact that when the ladies who worked at the flour company voted to use the name Betty, few of them could have known that by combining it with Bill's last name, that they were making up what would become one of the most popular—if fictional—names in America: Betty Crocker.

LITTLE-KNOWN FACT #74

The Dentist

Truth is, there aren't many people like Ed. But the world would be a better place if there were, that's for sure. No, Ed was a special kind of person. And to the veterans at the VA hospital, every Tuesday was special. Special because that's when Ed came to visit. Ed could always cheer up even the most discouraged man.

It was that wonderful jovial manner he had, along with that most distinctive voice and jolly sense of humor. Now, Ed's official reason for being at the VA hospital every Tuesday was as a dentist. Yes, Ed was a dentist and a darn good one. So good that he had been the head of oral surgery back in Oregon, where he graduated from dentistry school back in 1929. As a matter of fact, that's where Ed met his wife, Mildred. She was also in dental school and they graduated together. Yep, husband-and-wife dentists! The couple moved to southern California in 1937 and opened a practice together. But as it turned out, after only a couple of years, Ed turned the entire operation over to Mildred. He had another interest, but he never let this other interest get in the way of his weekly visits to our gallant men who were stuck in the VA hospital. Every Tuesday . . . there was Ed! And the men eagerly looked forward to his visits. Even if they weren't getting their teeth worked on.

You see, Ed would frequently sit down and just jaw with the veterans, sometimes for hours. And as I said, he was very entertaining. One of the men said, "An afternoon with Ed is better than a day at Disney." And I guess that was probably true.

Now, I'm sure you are asking why I'm bending your ear with a story of a nice bighearted dentist. Right?

Well, I have a good reason. Among other things, I have been telling you about a good friend of mine. Someone I have known for years. One of the best actors I've ever met. That's right, actor. Oh, you know him, this dentist! But it's a credit to Ed that you didn't know all the other wonderful things he did in his life.

It's a little-known fact that this talented man, this dentist, this good friend of mine, was in more than eighty feature films and over 150 television shows. And you still see him on the little screen today in dozens of reruns. His gravelly voice is as familiar as his face, but he is probably best known as lovable Uncle Joe on *Petticoat Junction*. The talented Edgar Buchanan. Yep, you'd never have guessed that he was really a dentist, would you? But the men at the VA can tell you. And so can I!

LITTLE-KNOWN FACT #75

A Little Light on the Subject

He knew he had something . . . and he was pretty sure it was going to be spectacular indeed. At last there was going to be something other than that smelly dangerous gas.

You see, long before most Americans were flipping a switch to light a room, oil lamps and natural gas were used. Gas companies were big business. They provided light, heat, and cooking fuel. In the middle of the nineteenth century, almost every large city had miles of underground gas pipes to provide fuel to businesses and residences for lamps and cooking.

It wasn't going to be long, though. Inventors from around the world were working on the question of electric illumination. Sir Humphry Davy was among the first who learned how to arc electric current between two posts. In 1844, Frenchman Jean Foucault followed suit by using that idea to light a large city square in Paris. But no one had made a device in which the electric arc was completely enclosed in glass, and safe enough to use in someone's home . . . until now.

This was a lightbulb. A simple device that housed a carbon filament and some gas. And was safe enough to use anywhere. He knew this would be big!

And I'm sure by now most of you are thinking, "This one's easy . . . ol' Dale is talking about Edison"—after all, Thomas Edison invented the lightbulb. That's what we were taught in grade school. And in fact Edison did get a patent on the lightbulb, but there's more. What Edison did differently was set up a system of electric distribution. If this invention was going to take off, he had to get it out of the lab and into homes and businesses.

Well, as you might guess, this took several years to accomplish, and Edison needed a little help. So he called on the only fella who knew as much about electric lights as he did—Joe Swan! With Joe's help, the two became partners in the distribution of light. Now, why did Edison pick Joe? Well, it seems that in England, Joe Swan had patented a carbon filament lightbulb . . . and he did it way before Edison.

It's a little-known fact that Thomas Edison did not invent the electric lightbulb. Sir Joseph William Swan did, ten months before Mr. Edison even announced his "discovery."

LITTLE-KNOWN FACT #76

Eat Your Heart Out, Calvin Klein

In the plains of Oklahoma, back in 1840, at the Fort Collins army post, something happened that is worth remembering. The commander of that post was stationed there with his wife and about 110 soldiers. The commander's wife was a proper lady from back east and wasn't overjoyed with this rather desolate assignment on the western frontier, but one thing that made her life a little more bearable was her daily walks. She dearly loved her walks and almost never missed one.

And that would have been fine, except for one thing. In addition to heat, Oklahoma has another distinguishing feature: wind. It's a wind that'll blow for days on end, and it doesn't slow down for man nor beast, nor even a lady on her daily stroll.

Now, what I'm trying to say as gently as possible is that during those promenades, the lady had a great deal of trouble keeping her skirt in place. And in those days, to show a little ankle—or perhaps more—was unthinkable. And among 110 bachelor soldiers on the post . . . well, let me just say that the commander had himself a discipline problem.

The commander explained to his wife that the walks were disruptive to the men and they would have to stop. But the walks were one of the very few pleasures she had, and she was not to be denied.

The commander was frustrated, but out of that frustration an idea was born. He came upon the idea of weighting the skirt just enough to keep it from blowing around. The most common commodity at an army post was bullets, so he had bullets sewn into the hem of this wife's skirt. It worked perfectly: She was delighted, and order was restored to the post.

Shortly thereafter the commander was assigned back east to Washington. There his wife regaled her society friends with the story of her weighted skirt. Not only that, she showed them some other skirts . . . and how gorgeously the fabric would drape and flow with the weighted hems. Overnight the weighted skirt became the rage of Washington society.

Now, she gave her husband full credit for the idea. And he came to be known as the inventor of the weighted skirt. He was a well-known flamboyant figure, accustomed to being noticed, but as a famous solider and Indian fighter, hardly as a clothes designer.

No, he was a leader of men, a general who fancied himself a battlefield hero. It is a little-known fact that people forgot about the general who invented the weighted skirt, but they certainly remember his name from another time in history: George Armstrong Custer.

LITTLE-KNOWN FACT #77

The Hypochondriac

You know folks, we remember what we want to remember! And that's especially true of famous people. Our heroes. We choose to remember their heroic feats and accomplishments . . . and I guess that's the way it should be. I mean, after all, most of us don't do anything that changes the course of human events. So when someone does, it's good and right that we remember them for their contribution to humankind. But sometimes the part that we forget is every bit as interesting.

Take the young woman who lay on her bed, her life hanging by a thread. She was waiting to die. But she didn't. She might as well have, though, because she became an invalid. Captive to what may be the worst thing a person could have . . . psychoneurosis.

That's right, she only believed she was sick.

The doctors couldn't find a thing wrong with her. And they tried. But one thing the doctors did notice was that virtually all of her illnesses followed family arguments. Oh, her symptoms were real enough. She was suffering, that's for sure. She had palpitations, shortness of breath, a racing heartbeat, and she got sick at the very sight of food.

If an unexpected or unwelcome visitor stopped by the house, the symptoms grew worse. She would develop debilitating headaches and chest pains. It got so bad, she finally moved out of her family home and into her own place. That in itself was very unusual for a single women in those days. But for the next three years, things were different for her. She found she had limitless energy and willingly took on new responsibilities. She found herself caring for the sick and injured. But remember, hers was a psychosis and she received no treatment for her own illness. Actually not much was known about it back then . . . and as you might expect, she relapsed after just three short years into her former state of imagined illnesses and waiting for death.

How are we so sure that her illness was imagined? Because she lived another fifty-seven years.

And why, you might ask, do we remember this hypochondriac today? Well, those three years that she was healthy and productive . . . those took place during the Crimean War. There she provided a service that gave women and the nursing profession respect worldwide.

It's a little-known fact that we have forgotten about the serious mental illness that she suffered from for most of her life . . . but we will always remember those three very loving and caring years in the life of Florence Nightingale.

LITTLE-KNOWN FACT #78

The One That Got Away

World War I was called the war to end all wars. More than twenty-five nations slugged it out in battles all over Europe, the Middle East, and North Africa. A total of sixty-five million soldiers fought in that war. Twenty-one million of them were wounded and nearly nine million killed.

Historians have spent a whole bunch of years trying to figure out what that war was all about. And many of them point straight to the emperor of Germany, Kaiser Wilhelm the Second, as the culprit who engineered the whole thing. Wilhelm was the grandson of William the First of Germany and Britain's Queen Victoria. He was well known to have a tendency to talk too much. To put it bluntly: He just couldn't keep his mouth shut. He seemed to know nothing about tact or diplomacy. London newspapers loved to repeat his outbursts. And when they reported him saying that the German people just didn't like the British, the ill will between the two countries shot up overnight.

Early on in his reign, world leaders criticized the kaiser for all the muscle he seemed to be flexing. Some say that Wilhelm didn't really want war, but he didn't seem to mind the idea if it would help him reach his most prized goal: to turn Germany into a great empire, a country to be reckoned with.

In the early 1900s, the kaiser stretched British nerves to the breaking point when he started building German battleships. The powers around him could only imagine one purpose for all those warships. England was so nervous that it made alliances with Russia and its old archenemy France. And, well, you probably know the rest. When the heir to the Austro-Hungarian throne was assassinated in 1914, war had come to Europe.

If you're up on your history, then you remember that America finally took up arms in that one when German submarines started attacking any ship in the Atlantic and, finally, sank the *Lusitania*, which just happened to be carrying U.S. citizens. That was in 1917, and by 1918 the Treaty of Versailles was signed and the great war was over. Wilhelm was forced to abdicate and when the peace treaty demanded that he be tried for promoting the war, he fled to Holland and sanctuary. And old Wilhelm lived just long enough to see Germany rise again during the Second World War. But there's a bit more to this story.

One of his more impetuous acts made him famous when he was still prince. It seems Buffalo Bill Cody had brought his Wild West show to Berlin and Wilhelm had a front-row seat. But the prince couldn't stand to sit on the sidelines, and so when one of the troupe's young performers got up to show off a rare shooting skill, he issued a challenge daring the young marksman to shoot the very cigarette he was smoking from his mouth. The shooter accepted the challenge. Wilhelm put the cigarette in its holder, then clenched it in his teeth. The marksman stepped back thirty paces and took aim. Well, the shot was made and Wilhelm lived to tell about it.

But later, the shooter wondered if a chance might have been missed to do the world a favor. "If my aim had been poorer," the Wild West performer recalled, "I might have averted the Great War."

It's a little-known fact that only one in a handful of sharpshooters could have made that shot and saved the kaiser's hide. And this time, the marksman happened to be a woman. And that would be, of course, America's very own Annie Oakley.

LITTLE-KNOWN FACT #79

The Kid!

He was known to almost every one of the poor and homeless from Broadway to Fifth Avenue. Well, they all knew him when they saw him anyway . . . but they really didn't know who he was.

What they did know is that when he came down the street, he would always pick out one or two to give money to. The poor and homeless who lived on the streets and in the alleys and slept in the doorways and subway stations just called him "the kid"! They could see him coming for blocks and they all ran to meet him when he came up the street. Some would actually shout, "Here comes the kid," while others wanted the kid all to themselves and didn't tell anyone when they saw him.

The kid.

They thought he was a rich kid because he always seemed to have money. But they couldn't have been more wrong. Oh, he was a kid all right, only eleven years old. And he did have money, but it was money he earned. And he would give it away to anyone he felt needed it. Especially other kids. And unlike the preachers and do-gooders who always wanted you to hear a lecture . . . the kid never said anything except that he wished they would go and get a good hot meal.

Paul Lancing was down on his luck and living on the street when one day the kid came by. Paul was too proud to beg, but the kid just came right up to him and said, "Could you use a couple of bucks?" Paul sure could. He had lost his job and was deeply depressed. But when he saw the generosity of that kid, he took courage. Paul used the money for bus fare and went to apply for a job. And he got it!

Ten years later, Paul was running a multimillion-dollar conglomerate.

Peter Jamison also accepted a couple of dollars and used it to buy some fruit from a vendor and sell it for a profit. It was small, but it was a start and hope. A few months later, Peter had a permanent stand in the prestigious marketplace and was doing very well.

And there were more . . . how many, we're not sure.

But it started from the kid.

His mother said that every day, he would take the money he made and split it in half. Then he promptly gave away half and kept the other half. I guess you could call it seed money, and it seemed to work all right, because that kid grew up to be very famous and very rich. And I understand that he kept up this practice throughout most of his life.

Well, it's a little-known fact that in 1896 in New York City, an eleven-year-old boy who couldn't stand to see people hungry or cold started a tradition that helped hundreds of people through some very rough times. And he never told any of them who he was . . . but we know the kid was the star of a major Broadway hit called *Peck's Bad Boy* . . . the very talented and generous George M. Cohan.

LITTLE-KNOWN FACT #80

Old Danny

He was an old man—at least that's what the soldiers at Fort Osage thought. Some even took to calling him "Old Danny" when they talked about him. "Old Danny said this," or "Old Danny did that."

Fact was, Old Danny had lots to say. He'd seen a lot in his life and he was about to see more. But he wasn't twenty years old anymore either, and a brief stop at the fort was good for the soul, not to mention the legs. Danny stayed for two weeks at Fort Osage, which is very near where Kansas City sits today. Most of the soldiers had even heard of Old Danny at one time or another. His exploits back east were—well, legendary!

And he would keep the soldiers on the edge of their seats for hours telling tales of his exploits from days gone by. And he wasn't done, not by a long shot. There was one more thing that Old Danny wanted to do. He'd wanted to do it for years, ever since he'd read a piece in newspaper years back, when a fella named Horace Greeley wrote, "Go west, young man!"

Well, okay, Danny wasn't all the young anymore, but he wasn't dead either, and that roving spirit that kept him going all his life was pushing him on again. He'd never seen the West and by gum, he was going to see it before he died.

At the fort he ran into a fellow named John Colter who had just returned from the land to the west. Colter talked of the area of the Platte River and the magnificence of the Rockies. And that made Danny all the more anxious. But John also talked about his run-in with hostile Indians; he'd just barely escaped with his life. He talked of unbelievably fierce weather and rugged terrain. John advised Old Danny to stay in Missouri where it was safe and he had all the comforts. But John didn't know Danny very well. For if he had, he would have known that his warnings were falling on deaf ears—so to speak.

You see, Danny was probably the best-known trailblazer of his day. Danny did make the trip to the West. He saw it all and came back to tell its tales. It's a little-known fact Danny had celebrated his eighty-second birthday before heading out across a two-thousand-mile journey that men in their twenties dreaded. But that was just the way old Daniel Boone was made.

LITTLE-KNOWN FACT #81

Captain's Leg

Wesley was the rarest of men. He was a creative fellow, that's for sure. A dreamer. But he also had a strong practical streak. Probably got that from his father, the police officer. Growing up, Wes was fascinated by airplanes and the future of aviation. He was determined to make his living from flying . . . and he did . . . but not like you might expect. He turned out to be quite a pilot.

While with the Army Air Corps in World War II, he was awarded the Distinguished Flying Cross for his service at Guadalcanal. He came home a hero, but so did a lot of men and women. As Wes would say, "They were all heroes." I'd have to agree. After the war, Wesley signed on as a commercial pilot. He was assigned to transatlantic flights, flying routes all over the world—Europe, Asia, Australia. It was on a late-night flight over the Syrian Desert that one of his engines caught fire. Almost before the captain could react, both engines were burning. The plane was going down and there wasn't a thing Wes or the rest of the crew could do about it. They crashed in the middle of the desert. Only eight people survived, and just one crew member, that was Wes . . . and he was injured. He knew it was up to him to save the rest. He had to get help. He remembered that just before the plane went down, he'd seen some lights far off in the distance. So he sent two of the passengers who could walk in that direction, not knowing how far it was, or how long they would take to reach those lights.

You might think that it had gotten about as bad as it could get—stranded at night in the middle of the Syrian Desert—but you'd be wrong. Out of nowhere came a band of desert nomads bent on looting the bodies and probably killing the rest. With every ounce of strength and courage he could muster, Wes faced down those cutthroats. He shouted and acted crazy and told those thieves they'd get those people's property only over his dead body! Even though he was outnumbered, they must've known he meant business, because they turned and left. Without taking a thing.

As morning came . . . so did rescue. The survivors told of Wes's courage in the face of that roving band of bandits. Once again, Wes was a hero. But that was enough of tempting the fates for Wesley. He decided that it was time to do something else . . . something a little safer. You remember I told you that Wes made his mark in the world from flying—and so he did!

But it was after he stopped flying aircraft and starting writing about them that the rest of us took notice. It's a little-known fact that the hero of that fateful flight would go on to create the most popular science fiction series of all time . . . *Star Trek*. The talented Gene Wesley Roddenberry.

LITTLE-KNOWN FACT #82

The Worst Postmaster in History

One thing has never changed about college students—they love to get letters from home. Usually because that's how they get their money.

You know the old story. The student writes, "Dear Mom and Dad, school is fine, I am in the glee club, met some nice friends, send money!" And Mom and Dad, being the loving folks that they are, and remembering when they were there themselves . . . send Johnnie or Susie a check. And you can bet that the kids watch that mailbox like a hawk. So when the mail system at the university gets messed up, the students are going to holler!

That's pretty much what happened at the University of Mississippi back in 1922. The school, like many other schools, had its own post office, complete with its own postmaster. And at this post office, that was Bill. Bill seemed a bright enough man, passed the civil service exam all right, and took the job. It was a bit surprising since Bill was a high school dropout and was rejected by the U.S. Army, but nonetheless, here he was at age twenty-four, postmaster. Problem was . . . he wasn't very good at it. Matter of fact, Bill was terrible! The mail would arrive by train and would be brought to Bill in the post office by another postal employee. It was Bill's job to sort the mail and get it ready for students to pick up from their individual mailboxes. Bill was often quite late for work, and when he did get there he'd just ignore the sacks of mail for hours on end. Students would come in to get their mail and it wouldn't be up yet. Just sitting in sacks on the floor.

Not only that, but Bill would frequently forget to sent outgoing mail to the train, so the students' letters to their parents would not get out for days on end. Students were furious, and they yelled at Bill for his laziness. That didn't help. Bill got mad and started throwing mail away. Even faculty mail and offical school mail was lost or delayed for weeks. Believe it or not, it took almost three years for postal officials to do anything about their rotten postmaster at the University of Mississippi. But eventually they did fire Bill.

And in a way, it's good for the rest of America that they did, because we would have missed out on some of the greatest literature of all time, if Bill was still posting letters. Because, it's a little-known fact that probably the worst postmaster in history was none other than William Faulkner!

LITTLE-KNOWN FACT #83

Crying Wolf?

It was almost inconceivable that it could have ever happened to begin with . . . much less again! Now I know that a lot of you are too young to remember, but I'm sure you've read about "the big broadcast" scare of October 30, 1938. It was called the War of the Worlds and it held parts of this country in a panic for hours. Here's what happened . . .

A talented young writer-director named Orson Welles was doing his weekly radio show. The show was very popular and listened to by thousands of people. Well, in the middle of the show, they interrupted the program to announce that an alien spacecraft had just landed in New Jersey and horrible Martian creatures were invading America.

Of course it was a ruse . . . a joke . . . meant to be entertainment. Welles even announced all that, at the beginning of the program and at each commercial break. But thousands didn't hear the announcements and thought the phony newscasts were real—and people were becoming hysterical. Some even believed that Martians were going to capture them and do terrible things . . . and tragically, took their own lives. Panic and terror spread across the Northeast and into parts of middle America and the South. Thousands of people were fleeing their homes for remote locations. Still others were barricading themselves and arming for a fight with the space creatures. People all over thought that America was being invaded . . . and all because of a radio program that was meant to be entertaining.

Evidently it was just a little too real. When it was over, Orson Welles was chastised by the press, the Congress, and even the president for playing such a hoax on the public, even though it was unintentional. And now . . . it appeared to be happening again. Welles was again in the middle of his network-wide radio broadcast reading a simple passage from Walt Whitman when an announcer broke in to tell America that we were being invaded.

Millions of listeners—remembering the great hoax of just three years before—did nothing. Even President Roosevelt heard the announcement in the White House and immediately fired off a terse wire telling Orson Welles to stop the nonsense before someone got hurt. The president accused him of crying wolf. But this time it wasn't Welles. It's a little-known fact, that it was during Orson Welles's broadcast that a real news reporter broke in and told the nation that the Japanese had just bombed Pearl Harbor. And for a while no one believed it!

LITTLE-KNOWN FACT #84

The Reluctant Revolutionary

Would he show up? That was something that the learned men at the science academy had to worry about every time they booked him to speak. Funny part was, he was one of the most requested speakers around—and still they could never depend on him to show up.

Many of the members didn't agree with him about his scientific findings, but they certainly wanted to hear his theories and see his data. Except for his habit of almost never showing up for his scheduled lectures. That in itself gave many of the scientists serious reason to doubt his findings. And they thought that not showing up was the height of disrespect. More often than not, he was sick—or thought he was, anyway.

You see, he suffered from a psychoneurosis, even before we knew much about the mental disease. Simply put, I guess, he was a hypochondriac. He believed he was sick, even when he wasn't. In addition, he often suffered from fainting spells, or near-fainting spells . . . and this most often occurred on the way to one of his lectures. He was well known for taking to his bed for months on end, and not seeing anyone at all, friend or foe. And it gets worse. On the very rare occasion when he did actually make it to a scheduled lecture . . . he had a terrible stutter. His speech was halting and full of stammers. He had an especially hard time with scientific terminology. So much so that many of his colleges thought that he either didn't know what he was talking about, or just flat didn't believe his theories himself. Of course he did believe his own theories. Or did he?

There is some evidence to show that he didn't actually believe everything that he brought to the scientific society. Actually, for someone who was about to change the world and the way we think, he couldn't have been a worse representative for his own body of evidence. In the end, he simply became a recluse . . . and for nearly twenty-five years refused to see anyone at all. Strange behavior for a man who proposed to change our world as we knew it. Well, it's a little-known fact that this stuttering, bedridden reclusive hypochondriac was the man who brought the world the Theory of Evolution . . . Charles Darwin. And why might he not have believed it all himself? Well, because he married his first cousin!

LITTLE-KNOWN FACT #85

The Volunteer

I know you've heard of it, but I wonder if you have any idea how intense it really was. I'm talking about the Battle of Bull Run. Well, I guess I could be talking about any battle of any war, really. They're all bad. No good comes from all that killing and maiming of other people.

Yes, I guess you could say that front-line battles are some of the most traumatic times anyone could face. And they often bring out the best and worst in a person. One thing is for sure—if you live, you'll know what you're made of. That was certainly the case for Harry T. Buford. I guess most of us would say that Harry was made of the right stuff. Harry had been in a number of battles during the war, and this battle, Bull Run, was yet one more in which he was to face his fears and draw on his inner strengths to get him through. Those inner strengths had served him well over the past few years.

In battle after battle, in hand-to-hand combat, and even charging in the face of enemy fire, Harry had more than held his own. In fact, he was considered one of the best and bravest soldiers in the division. And what's so funny about all this is that Harry didn't have to be there. He wasn't a conscript, he wasn't drafted or forced to serve. He had volunteered and he could leave any time he wanted to. Yes, he could. You see, Harry knew something that no one else knew . . . and if he was to tell, the army would send him home in a second. But he kept his mouth shut, and served honorably in his division. A division commanded by no less than Stonewall Jackson himself. And like all the officers and men in the division, Jackson had seen for himself the courage, bravery, and determination of Harry Buford. Ol' Stonewall both praised and decorated Harry on four separate occasions for his bravery and leadership in battle. Harry was a hero and leader of men. But what Jackson didn't know . . . what no one knew . . . was that Harry hid every night. Not from fear of battle . . . no, he hid from discovery.

I told you that Harry didn't have to be there, and it's true. You see, Harry volunteered for duty after a loved one was killed in the war. It was Harry's husband. It's a little-known fact that Harry Buford, four-time decorated battle-field hero, was in reality Loretta Velasquez . . . a woman!

LITTLE-KNOWN FACT #86

Wanted: Dead or Alive

You know, folks, history has some funny twists and turns in it . . . and I guess that's what makes it so interesting.

Sometimes people are not what they seem. Or they just flat out change. If you think about it a spell, you can probably think of someone you thought was not the kind of person you wanted to associate with . . . only to find out later that you had misjudged. Or as is often the case, the other way around. That may well have been the case with Allan. Why? Because when this Scottish boy from the Highlands was back in his native country, he was an outlaw. Considered a criminal. He was a rebellious political activist. And not just the kind who went around carrying signs and doing sit-ins. No, not Allan. He was an extremist. Oh, he had a good reason: His country was trying to gain independence from England, and he was one of the fiery leaders of the rebellion. There was a price on his head.

Now this was a few years ago, 1839 to be exact. Allan seemed to have a special talent. He was developing some special tactics for defeating the ruling British class. He was developing some highly skilled infiltration and surveillance techniques, which he would frequently use against the Brits. He was able to get himself into some of the most secret and high-security areas and spy on his adversaries, delivering vital information back to his side. He developed sophisticated covert operations that had never been thought of before. I mean, this guy made Delilah look like an amateur. But eventually, the heat got too much for Allan and he fled Scotland for America. Wouldn't you know!

But all those highly developed skills didn't go to waste. Oh no! This time on the other side of the law, though. He used them to track and catch some of the most notorious criminals in our society—the James brothers, John Wesley Hardin, and more. He recruited men and trained them in how to protect trains and stagecoaches. Railroads hired him to track down and stop train robbers . . . and he did!

He was even asked to start the Secret Service.

Yep, it's a little-known fact that the man who started the biggest and most successful detective and security agency in the world, which is still in business today, learned his skills for criminal purposes in his own homeland . . . the wily and effective Allan Pinkerton!

LITTLE-KNOWN FACT #87

The Surfer Dude

Mel had to admit it was one of the most beautiful places he had ever seen in his life. And he had seen a lot. He had traveled around the world and visited many places, but, yes, Hawaii had to be one of the prettiest. He liked it even better than Tahiti. And he didn't think he would ever like any place more than Tahiti. But he did.

And he was fascinated with that thing the natives were doing. Surfing, they called it!

He had never seen that before. These ingenious folks had a board that they had smoothed down, and they were riding the surf with it. Now, I know we don't think there is much unusual about surfing these days, but when Mel first saw the natives of Hawaii doing this, it was new and different. Mel had heard of this sport from his fellow sailors, and was anxious to see it for himself.

Yes, Mel was a sailor. He had signed on to a freighter some time ago and had spent the last six years sailing around the world. He loved the places he got to see and visit and he learned something in each place. But this was special. He couldn't resist, so you guessed it—he decided to try surfing for himself. Well, the surfboards weren't as sophisticated or advanced as they are today. And they didn't have those little tie ropes that keep the board from running away when you fall off the thing. So Mel spent quite a bit of time chasing his board. But eventually he did get the "hang" of it and he became something of a good surfer. He stayed in Hawaii several months and surfed every day. He loved it and couldn't wait to bring the sport back to America. And he did!

He brought three surfboards back with him when he returned home; he was just sure that the sport would take over America the way it had Hawaii. Well, he was right, it did catch on here, but not in his lifetime. Or for another 150 years, really. You see, part of the problem was that Mel lived in Massachusetts. The water there was and is pretty cold, and wet suits hadn't been invented yet. Not to mention that Massachusetts really doesn't have the waves for surfing. So a few people laughed at Mel when he demonstrated his newfangled sport, but nobody was really interested. And I guess in a way that was okay.

Because a century or so later another fella did bring surfing to America in a big way. And Mel, he went back to sailing . . . and writing. Yes, he loved to write. That's how we know about this surfboard business. He doesn't get credit for the surfing craze in America, but as far as we can tell, he was the very first to introduce it here.

It's a little-known fact that the man who brought the first surfboard to this country and tried to introduce it as a recreational activity will never be known for that, but he will always be remembered as one of the most respected writers of all time. Because he created one of the most respected books of all time. One that is to this day required reading in most schools. A story of the sea . . . and a harsh captain . . . and a whale. *Moby-Dick.* By the author and one-time surfer Herman Melville.

LITTLE-KNOWN FACT #88

The Odd Couple

Evidently it was more than the guests could stand. All that arguing and loud talking going on half the night. That is, if we are to believe the written accounts of the event. What was it? Well, two men arguing—or *discussing,* as they later insisted—over whether to sleep with the window open or closed. One fellow said that the fresh air did wonders for your health and made you sleep like a baby. The other fellow was just as convinced that the night air would make you sick; besides, it was cold.

Well, that they could both agree on. It was cold. It was New England in the middle of the winter, and I can tell you it is cold at night. Well, believe it or not, this loud discussion went on to the wee hours of the morning, much to the discomfort of the other guests. And it was accompanied by a great deal of noisy window opening and closing.

You wouldn't think that this would cause other guests to lose sleep, would you? But this all happened back in the late 1770s and the traveler's accommodations, such as they were, were—well, roadside inns really. Not much more than a big house, and sometimes not that big, just set on the side of a horse path. The inn usually had about three or four guest rooms and a dining room; bathrooms were out back. And because there were almost always more travelers than rooms and beds, guests often had to share a bed.

This was especially true if they were traveling together, but often even strangers had to sleep in the same bed or face a cold hard floor. That was no problem with these fellas—they not only knew each other, they were friends, and they were traveling together. But evidently they didn't discuss window arrangements before they left. Well, the guests were complaining about the window banging and loud talking. No one in the place was getting any sleep. Finally it woke the innkeeper, too.

And he went up to the room about midnight to ask these fellows to calm down and let the other guests sleep. They assured him that they would. But a short time later, loud discussion was heard again. The innkeeper had to go up three more times that night to shush the men. He muttered to himself that he should have known better than to put those two in the same room. After all, they were both pretty well known for their talking and strong opinions. But this window business was carrying things a bit too far.

Well, it's a little-known fact that that keeper of a small roadside inn had to four times go and shush and threaten to throw out two of our nation's founding fathers and greatest heroes: John Adams and Benjamin Franklin.

Maybe we can remember that the next time our kids are a little too rambunctious.

LITTLE-KNOWN FACT #89

The Sports Writer

One hundred twenty-five thousand dollars! Just for one man to play baseball. I know that doesn't sound like much today, but in 1920 it was—well, it was more than anyone could ever have imagined a baseball player could make.

It happened when the Boston Red Sox sold the great Babe Ruth, to the New York Yankees. And the Babe became an idol, a hero . . . more loved than even the president.

And just like today, there were a lot of people who agreed and a lot of folks who thought that amount of money was just outrageous. That was certainly the case with Bill. He was the sports editor and chief writer for the *Morning Telegraph.* And he did certainly think that $125,000 was excessive for a ball player. And he said so (!) in his column. Again and again.

Now, don't misunderstand—Bill loved sports. That's why he was a sportswriter. And from the end of World War I through the 1920s, America was having a sports explosion. Not only was the biggest salary deal in history just made, but professional football was taking off with a superstar recruit named Red Grange. Walter Hagen was propelling America to world dominance in professional golf, and Big Bill Tilden and Helen Wills proved that

Americans could hold their own on the Wimbledon tennis courts, right along with all those snooty Brits. And Bill loved all of it.

But $125,000 was ridiculous, and he said so.

Well, it seems that the great Babe Ruth took exception to Bill harping over and over about his salary. Other writers had expressed their disapproval, once or twice. But they quit. Of course the Babe did have to call a couple of them and explain that if they didn't quit, he would come and explain things to them personally. And since the Babe had a reputation for being as fisty and hardhitting off the field as on, most reporters . . . got the message.

Except Bill.

He kept right on expressing his disapproval. He just couldn't believe that paying an athlete this much money was good for sports. Well, guess what? The Babe had enough and called Bill. He threatened that a personal visit might be in order. But Bill wasn't a bit afraid. He told the great Ruth to come on. Well, that did it. The Babe packed a bag and hopped a train to—well, discuss the matter with Bill. But while on the train, Ruth was talking to a fella who was reading one of Bill's columns. The fellow asked Ruth if he knew who Bill was. Ruth didn't!

And when this stranger told Babe who Bill really was . . . Ruth got off the train at the next station and went back home. Now, who on earth had a reputation that would have turned Babe Ruth around in this tracks?

Babe had heard of the man all right, most folks had, but Babe thought he was still out in Kansas. It's a little-known fact that the only man whom Babe Ruth was not willing to take on was the ex-marshal and onetime fastest gun in the West, now a sportswriter: William Barclay Masterson. Bat Masterson. I think I would have turned around, too!

LITTLE-KNOWN FACT #90

There's a Spy in My Mouth!

Californians were a little paranoid. Now, some of you may not think that's so unusual, but this time they had a reason. After all, a Japanese submarine had been spotted off the Santa Barbara coast and someone had seen a zero flying near Santa Monica. Japanese Americans had been sent to interment camps at Manzanar and everybody was suspicious of everybody else. And one particular California woman had double reason to be nervous. Not only did she worry about the Japanese, but she had an appointment with her dentist . . . and she hated the dentist.

But even in the middle of a war life must go on—even for someone with bad teeth. And she did have awful teeth. What's worse, her job required her to have a great smile, so teeth were important. She spent the better part of the day in the dentist's chair getting her teeth drilled—both uppers and lowers—and temporary fillings made of lead put in while he finished the permanent ones.

Yes, I said lead. That's what they used to make them out of before we learned better.

A few nights later, while driving back to her ranch after work, she heard music. She even recognized the song and she reached down to turn off the radio, but the radio wasn't on. The music got louder and she noticed her mouth vibrating with the rhythm of the music. Then, as quickly as it came, the music faded out.

Fairly sure she was going crazy, she hesitated to tell anybody about it, but the next day she decided to trust someone and mentioned it to her very good friend Buster. He asked her if she was at the intersection of Moorpark and Coldwater and if she had any lead fillings. Well, needless to say, she was amazed. But he only laughed and told her that another friend of his had picked up the radio station near Moorpark and Coldwater through the fillings in his teeth.

Well, now she was intrigued. She started driving around trying to pick up the station again, but with no luck. She had just about forgotten about the whole episode when one night—in a totally different location—she picked up not music, but Morse code. Can you imagine? Her mouth started jumping, with *de-de de-de* bouncing off her molars.

The next day she told the authorities, and they called in the FBI. Sure enough, the authorities ferreted out a secret underground Japanese radio station in somebody's basement. It turned out that their gardener was a spy.

I know it sounds like the plot of an *I Love Lucy* episode, but I can assure you it's true. And what happened to that California woman who hated going to the dentist? Well, she really never lost the fear of the dentist. But she did go on to become known and loved for so many other things— including *I Love Lucy*!

It's a little-known fact that Lucille Ball's bad teeth may have influenced the outcome of World War II. And the friend who told her she wasn't crazy? Well, that was Buster Keaton.

LITTLE-KNOWN FACT #91

The Home Front

One thing about a war—patriotism is usually at an all-time high. And that's the way it was in World War II. Everyone wanted to be part of the war effort, even those whose day-to-day duties lay far from the front.

And that's kind of where our story starts. At a fashionable dinner party one night in 1940, a popular composer named George Antheil was doing his part by performing for a benefit. That night, his inspiration had come from a beautiful young Viennese woman whom his hostess had seated right next to him. She was lovely! Without a doubt one of the most beautiful women George Antheil had ever seen. And he wasn't the only one who thought so . . . the young woman was attracting the attention of nearly everyone at the party.

Even though Mrs. Markey was new to America, she shared in America's patriotic sentiments. She had even been thinking about a military innovation, which she thought might help the Allies win the war. She shared her thoughts with the musician. Antheil listened intently as she described her idea: a device that would send radio commands to torpedoes in coded patterns, enabling the weapon to be guided without being jammed by enemy. The idea was a good one, and there was something about it Antheil knew rang a bell with him. But he just couldn't put his finger on it.

Suddenly the answer came to him. Player pianos! Of course! The beautiful young Mrs. Markey had been describing the design for a variable radio tune, whose frequency was changed from time to time by punched instructions in a belt. The design was almost identical to that of a player piano. The two might actually be on to something.

That evening was the beginning of an intense collaboration between a radiantly beautiful Viennese inventor and an American composer. The team stayed together for two years, working out problems with the design and re-thinking their project. And finally—in 1942—they were ready. They applied for and received a patent.

Antheil sometimes wondered if his partner's inspiration came from her past. She had, after all, been briefly married to Friedrich Mandl, one of the world's leading munitions tycoons. That was, of course, before she came to the States to start her new career. And she did pretty well with that, too. I believe I already mentioned that she was quite a looker, called by some "the world's most beautiful woman." And Hollywood's most glamorous star. It's a little-known fact that the woman who invented the radio coding device that so significantly helped the Allies win the war was the lovely and elegant film star Hedy Lamarr.

LITTLE-KNOWN FACT #92

The Hand of Destiny

The train was late . . . again! Trains never really ran on time, but with the war—the Civil War—in full furor, the trains ran later and later. Not to mention slow. Most trains only chugged along at about twenty or twenty-five miles an hour. It was faster than a horse, but not by much.

On top of everything else, with shipping soldiers and equipment to the war and the wounded back home, traveling by train was more of a challenge than anything else. It was a real frustration to Robert all right. He had just finished conducting some very special business for his father in Jersey City and needed to get back home and report. He noticed that there were a number of important people all waiting for the same train.

For example, there was that famous actor that Robert recognized from several stage plays he had seen at the theater. He was tempted to walk up and introduce himself and tell the famed actor how much he enjoyed his last performance. But it was late at night and everyone looked tired. And Robert—well, he didn't want to bother the famous man. A large crowd gathered next to the train all eager to get one of the few beds left on the incoming Pullman sleeper.

Robert noticed a number of government officials in the crowd—not necessarily unusual, since the train would stop in the nation's capital. Robert was trying to make his way toward the platform conductor, hoping to buy a sleeping compartment. But the crowd had grown so large that he was forced to the edge of the platform. Suddenly he could hear the whistle of the approaching train. In its excitement, the crowd surged, and Robert was forced closer to the edge and the tracks. Suddenly the crowd surged again and Robert felt himself pushed right into the path of the oncoming train. He fought to get back onto the platform, but there was no room. He thought he was a goner.

Then in a flash he felt a hand grab him by the collar of his coat and pull him back onto the platform. He was saved from almost sure death. When he turned around to thank his rescuer, he recognized the famous actor he had seen earlier. It was Edwin Booth. He and his brother John Wilkes Booth were probably the most famous actors in Washington.

It's a little-known fact that Edwin Booth saved Robert from almost certain death that late night on the train platform . . . and who could know that not more than a year and a half later, Edwin's brother John would shoot the president, thereby ending forever Robert Todd Lincoln's days in the White House with his father.

Robert Todd Lincoln was the only son of President Abraham Lincoln and Mary Todd Lincoln.

LITTLE-KNOWN FACT #93

That Daring Young Man on the Flying Trapeze

Jack wanted to be a doctor. Or at least he thought he did. He and his father had discussed it and decided that medicine would be the career for him. Jack grew up in Chicago in the late 1920s.

One day he met a young fellow named Bobby. Bobby was about the same age as Jack. They seemed to get along, until Bobby's father came around one day and Jack and his whole family realized that Bobby was the son of the notorious mobster Al Capone.

Well, I don't think it was because of that incident, but whatever the reason, Jack was shipped off to Florida to live with his aunt and study to be a doctor. Jack took his studies seriously for a short time, until one day, through a friend, he was offered the chance to learn a new skill: the flying trapeze. He wasn't exactly sure that flying, as the trapeze artists call it, was exactly what he wanted to do, either, but he had to admit it was fun, and when he got to perform in a show, he loved the attention.

Well, that was the end of his medical career. The flying act was booked to appear at the 1934 World's Fair, and Jack and the whole flying troop knew that they would have to develop something special for that appearance. They worked on a number of different ideas, until one day, two of the fliers almost collided in midair. At the last second, Jack changed his grip and sailed over the top of his fellow flier. That was it. They had found their special move, called the Passing Leap.

Now, if you have been to the circus and watched the amazing trapeze artists, you know that today, this maneuver—one man leaving the trapeze and flying toward the catcher, while at the same time another person leaves the pedestal, and they cross over the top of one another in midair—is fairly commonplace. As a matter of fact, the Passing Leap is one of the most popular stunts among trapeze artists today. Virtually all of them do it.

But I'll bet you didn't know that Jack was the one to develop it. And if you didn't know that, then you probably don't know what else Jack did. Well, it's a little-known fact that the trapeze flier who thought he was going to be a doctor and later developed one of the most popular moves on a trapeze was . . . Jack Carlton Moore. That's right: Clayton Moore, whom we all have come to know and love as the Lone Ranger!

LITTLE-KNOWN FACT #94

Two-Gun Hart

Vincent was born in Brooklyn in 1892. From his early boyhood, he knew he was not destined to live in a big city with giant skyscrapers and crowded streets. Determined to escape the concrete canyons and dirty air, he left home at the age of sixteen and headed west.

Anxious for adventure, Vincent joined the circus and traveled throughout the West. He was fascinated by Native Americans and studied their ways. His journey through the West was interrupted, however, by World War I. He joined the army and shipped out for France, where his excellent marksmanship—which he had learned in the circus—quickly got him promoted to first lieutenant.

Vincent was to use his skill with a gun for the rest of his life. When the war was over, he hopped a train to Nebraska, where he soon became a Prohibition enforcement officer. By this time, Vincent had decided to change his name to something with a more western sound to it. He was now Richard Hart.

And it wasn't long before he became known as Two-Gun Hart. You see, in addition to busting up illegal stills, he also helped keep the peace in the frontier towns by arresting horse thieves and other criminals.

Two-Gun Hart and his new bride, Kathleen, shared a fascination with the American Indian culture. They and their four sons lived among the Sioux and Cheyenne tribes and were close friends with the tribal leaders. Two-Gun and all the boys even learned several Indian languages.

His fame as a lawman and expert marksman was the reason the Secret Service hired him as an extra bodyguard for President Calvin Coolidge whenever the president was on official trips out west.

Yep, Two-Gun Hart had come a long way from a crowded tenement back in Brooklyn. But he never forgot the big family he came from and would occasionally travel to Chicago to visit with his two brothers Ralph and John. And even though they became close friends again, Richard Hart told his two brothers to tell their fourth brother that if he ever visited Nebraska, Two-Gun Hart would arrest him and throw him in jail the minute he crossed the state line.

You see, it's a little-known fact that one of the most famous lawmen of the Old West, who changed his name from Vincent—well, actually, Vincenso—to Richard, was the brother of America's most notorious gangster, Al Capone.

LITTLE-KNOWN FACT #95

The Weirdest War in History

It was probably the strangest war anyone has ever been involved in—as far as I can tell anyway. The War of 1812 started on the high seas. You've heard of getting shanghaied. Well, if you'd been an American sailor back then, the odds were pretty high that you'd find yourself in just that position. The British insisted that they could take all Englishmen serving on American ships. And they sure didn't mind helping themselves to most of the Americans while they were at it!

Fact is, thousands of U.S. citizens were forced to work on British ships, which were notorious for their cruel discipline and wretched living conditions. American diplomats protested time and time again, but it all fell on deaf ears.

Then there was the trade problem. The French wanted the Americans to quit trading with the English. And the English wanted them to quit trading with the French. And so they both started blocking American ships from each other's ports. And the Americans were still having to defend their own boundaries at home: The French were to the north, Spain still had control of Florida, and the English were stirring up hostile American Indians all over the place. Americans found themselves fighting all sorts of people. But oddly enough, some of the same groups proved to be America's strongest allies. Before the war was over, even pirates would be talked into fighting for the United States.

This was the war where the British marched straight to the White House, stacked the furniture in the parlor, and set it on fire. Funny thing was, before the English burned down Washington, D.C., most of Congress was all for moving the capital. They just couldn't stand that swampy land and mosquitoes. But once the English burned it, Congress was dead set on staying put. It was the war where Francis Scott Key penned the national anthem and the country adopted the nickname "Uncle Sam." And it was the war where the government went broke halfway before it was over.

But probably the strangest thing about this war had to do with the pitifully poor communications. Two days before Congress voted to fight, the British agreed to one of America's biggest demands. But that message reached James Madison too late. War had already been declared.

And the ending of that war—well, it was an awful lot like its beginning.

It's a little-known fact that the most famous battle of the War of 1812—the Battle of New Orleans—was fought about two weeks after the Americans had signed a peace treaty with England. Andrew Jackson and his army found that out a month too late.

LITTLE-KNOWN FACT #96

Things Change

His name was White Bull and he was a chief of the Teton Lakota. Actually he accomplished quite a bit in his life. In his own words: "First I followed the way of my fathers, then the way of the white man."

And maybe we don't have a full appreciation of what it took to make such a dramatic change. A change from a way that had been taught at the lodge poles and campfires since the beginning of time. Then, suddenly to take on a whole new way of existing. The old ways passing away, he had to learn new customs, new language, new procedures, and new laws. He was the son of Good Feather Woman and nephew of Sitting Bull.

As a young man, he was a warrior, and a brave one. He fought the fight against the Flatheads. He fought in the war against the Omahas. He fought the Battle of Greasy Creek. He stole ponies from his Indian enemies and grabbed his share of squaws from neighboring tribes. And he fought in the most famous battle of all. But the time of the warrior was growing short, and White Bull could see it was so. He led his people to a safer life, in the ways of the white settlers. He was elected chief of the Teton Lakota.

Once a chief, White Bull was selected to become an Indian policeman, and he served well. He was made a tribal judge and chairman of the tribal council. He was later selected to be a government policeman and, when some trouble with the Utes arose, he went in and arrested those who'd caused the problems and calmed the whole situation down. And maybe most amazing of all, Chief White Bull was given a commission in the U.S. Army. And that was something that was seldom done, especially if you had killed another regular commissioned army officer . . . which he had.

You see, it's a little-known fact that this forgotten leader of the Lakota Sioux had done something that will live in infamy. Many years before, at the Battle of the Little Big Horn, it was a young White Bull who jumped off his horse and in hand-to-hand combat killed Colonel George Armstrong Custer.

LITTLE-KNOWN FACT #97

Getting Their Feet in the Door

Anyone who has ever taken a pen in hand to write professionally will tell you an editor is the bane of every author. Every writer I've ever met, and I've met a bunch of them, can show you a boxful of rejection notices. It's hard to believe that there are editors who've turned down the talents of people like Clancy, Michener, Faulkner, and Sheldon . . . but there are!

And I'm not just talking about novels. No, magazines and newspapers too. Some of our best and most prolific writers share their talent in the monthly periodicals that we find on the magazine rack at the grocery store.

Well, that was not the case with Julie. That's what his friends called him—Julie. Actually Julie was a well-known writer. He was one of the founding writers of the famed *New Yorker* magazine. He was a regular featured columnist in the *St. Louis Dispatch*, the *Los Angeles Times*, the Hearst newspapers, and more. Julie's columns were known for their witty satire and sharp insights into American life. People loved his columns.

But Julie understood about how other writers struggled. You see, he didn't have his writing job because he was such a good writer, although he was; no, he got these writing gigs because he was a star. A screen legend. Editors and publishers begged for his stuff. And he delivered!

And he sympathized with how other good writers struggled to get published. Julie knew that if writers were given a chance, people would realize their talent. So when the demands of his other career got to be too much and he couldn't get a column out in time, he would often secretly give an unknown writer his byline. Yep, he would allow an unknown writer to produce his column and Julie would submit it under his name. And it would get published. And when the public demanded more, Julie would tell the editors that it had come from another writer and how they were passing up on some great talents.

Julie did this for some of the best and most loved writers of our time, like famed playwright Arthur Sheckman. And you can bet your life, the writers were thrilled to get a chance. Julie never did tell us how many writers he helped in this way—it was his secret—but we know there were a lot. And he never took credit for being the one to bring their talents to public attention. No, he was satisfied with the attention he got from his other career . . . movies and television.

It's a little-known fact that the writer who helped so many other young writers gain fame and find a career was none other than Julius H. Marx—better known as Groucho!

LITTLE-KNOWN FACT #98

The Itty-Bitty Revolution

It wasn't that long ago really—1968—and America was undergoing many changes. We were at war in Vietnam, and young peaceniks mounted a political movement to nominate Eugene McCarthy for president. Students took over Columbia University and held the whole place hostage for weeks and weeks. The Democratic Convention was disrupted by protests, and the radical SDS were talking about revolution.

And not just here in America. Students in France did make a revolution that lasted for about two weeks.

It was a time when hippies were in full bloom and flower children were marching in their ragged bell-bottoms and tie-dyed shirts. It was a time when long hair was an expression of rebellion and grown men held down screaming boys and shaved their heads. And a new invention was about to change the world.

Do you remember the computers in those days? Let me guess . . . you're saying, "What computers," right? Well, it was a long time before personal computers, that's for sure. But some computers did exist. Remember UNIVAC? Oh, we had computers, but they were huge! In those days, if you wanted to do some computer work, you had to go to a computer center at a big university or a big corporation. You had to punch up cards . . . remember "Do not fold, spindle or mutilate"?

But in the fall of 1968, not long after the riots at the Democratic Convention in Chicago, a bright young fella named Douglas C. Engelbart went to San Francisco to the fall joint computer conference to show a new idea. Remember, this was sixteen years before the first personal computer. For his demonstrations Douglas hooked up with what was then a big mainframe computer at Stanford University—all of 192 kilobytes—twenty-five miles away. He had what he called the first "user-friendly information access systems," something like what we call Windows today.

But he had another gadget that absolutely stopped the show! He called it an "x-y position indicator." With this little gadget, everyday people were about to find that they, too, could use a computer, something that only programming experts had been able to do so far. People gathered from all over the convention center to see this little bitty marvel of technology.

It's a little-known fact that in 1968 Douglas C. Engelbart invented his x-y position indicator and the world of computing changed forever—so much so that almost every computer in the world now has one. You've got one! You use it all the time. Oh, yes, you do! That x-y position indicator is what you probably call . . . a mouse.

LITTLE-KNOWN FACT #99

The Real Doogie Howser, M.D.?

Imagine for a moment, won't you? You are a doctor. Matter of fact, you are considered a genius. You graduated from medical school at the top of your class. You're a physician, a healer, a skilled surgeon . . . ready to help humankind with your extraordinary talent and skill. And you can't get any patients! Not a one!

Wally could have told you what it was like. It happened to him. Some people thought it was his beard, or lack of it! You see, Wally couldn't grow one. He was one of those fellows whose whiskers just didn't come in. He tried, but it was just . . . well, peach fuzz.

One problem with growing a full beard was that Wally was young. Very young! I already told you he was a genius, and I wasn't kidding. He graduated from medical school at the age of seventeen. And if that wasn't enough, he became a licensed surgeon the next year.

The next couple of years he served on the Brooklyn Board of Health and the New York Board of Health. Then he decided that he would open a private practice in 1874. The baby-faced Wally was approaching twenty-two years old. He was a skilled doctor and surgeon. But because he looked like he was still in high school, no one would believe him. No one trusted this . . . kid . . . to treat them. Back then most men had beards. But try as he may, Wally's beard just wouldn't grow. Oh, he'd get a few straggling hairs to pop out, but he looked ridiculous. He was just one of those men who couldn't grow a beard. And a baby face also meant that he didn't have any patients.

That was a problem, you see, because Wally was also in love with Emile Lawrence—a lovely young woman who pretty much had her hat tipped in Wally's direction too. But Wally was broke. No patients equaled no money. No money meant no wife. Wally seriously considered quitting medicine altogether so he could get a job and marry Emile. In absolute frustration, Wally joined the army as a surgeon.

And it's a good thing for all of us that he did. You see, he then used his genius to become one of the first bacteriologists. Then director of the U.S. Army commission that ultimately ended the yellow fever epidemic.

Yep, it's a little-known fact that the baby-faced doctor who couldn't get a patient because he couldn't grow a beard and nearly quit medicine completely became one of this country's most respected doctors. He's even got a huge medical center named after him. You hear about it all the time. Whenever our president has to go see the doctor, he goes to . . . Walter Reed Medical Center!

LITTLE-KNOWN FACT #100

From a Different Point of View

Where do ideas come from? I suppose it would be obvious that many of them come from the academic environment of the great universities. A genius is kind of like a dry bale of hay, just waiting for that spark to light the fire.

Well, folks, one of the most important inventions in the

history of humankind came to one brilliant young fellow while he was looking at the back end of a horse.

That's the way the story goes. He was tilling a potato field with a horse-drawn harrow on his dad's farm in Idaho. He kept going back and forth and back and forth. That motion, that back and forth across the field, ignited an idea in this young man that would eventually change our entire society.

He used that very same horse to ride four miles each day to the nearest school. And it's good for us that he did. Because that's where he met Mr. Justin Tolman, his chemistry teacher.

Mr. Tolman turned out to be that lightning bolt that turned on the fire in this shy little farm boy. Mr. Tolman could tell early on that the young man had a keen interest in science. So he gave him private instructions and even allowed him to sit in on the senior classes.

How could they possibly have known that the two of them would be in court in the years to come, having to prove that a most remarkable invention had started in a cold Idaho schoolroom?

Well, because few people in Idaho, or on the planet earth, for that matter, understood some of his ideas, the young man moved on. He was smart enough to get into Brigham Young University at the age of sixteen, where not all of the professors were able to follow him when he told them about the idea he'd had, back behind that horse, when he was fifteen.

Finally, at the ripe old age of twenty-one, he arrived in San Francisco with a new wife and some investors. On September 7, 1927, he took a pane of glass, painted it black, and scratched a line on it. No one in the room knew they were looking at the future.

Well, the government finally awarded our young farm boy the patent . . . but only after his high school teacher, Mr. Tolman, testified that yes, the shy student had explained his theory when he was all of fifteen.

There is a statue of him in the rotunda of the U.S. Capitol. Millions of tourists, many who could not possibly imagine life without his invention, stroll by without taking notice. If they do stop to read the plaque, some find his name a little comical. They might find it hard to believe that Philo T. Farnsworth knew that if you sent light back and forth across a piece of glass—just like that plow across that field—that you would have television.

LITTLE-KNOWN FACT #101

For the Love of Ice Cream

He was born Ole Hakonsen, but that only lasted until he was five years old. That's when his parents came to this country and they took the surname of the farm where they worked. When the family came across to this promised land on a freighter, it was clear even then what interested Ole the most. On that journey across the ocean, he spent all his free time in the engine room. When others were enjoying an ocean cruise, Ole was getting dirty and greasy in a hot steamy room, five decks below the sunshine and fresh air. His parents settled in Wisconsin and sent Ole to school, but he left grade school early—it was too easy for him and his mind wandered.

He left home and worked in factories up and down the Midwest from Pittsburgh to Chicago. In 1900, at the age of twenty-three, Ole returned to Wisconsin and set up a pattern-making shop in Milwaukee. He didn't meet with great success as a pattern maker, but he did gain some local notoriety as an engineer. And that's not all—he was also becoming known as an eccentric.

You see, Ole had read about the internal combusion engine when it was still in the experimental stages in Germany, being used on the first horseless carriages, back in the 1890s. And now that he had a shop of his own, he wanted to build some, too. So for his business he did engineering odd jobs, but in his spare time he built horseless carriages. He test-drove them, too . . . up and down the normally quiet streets of Milwaukee, much to the consternation of his neighbors.

Now, the office manager of Ole's little pattern-making shop was a lovely lass named Bess Cary, and as you might guess, she and Ole fell in love and became engaged in 1906. One of the things that Bess loved was going on a romantic picnic . . . and not just any picnic. No, a picnic on an island on a lake.

Well, Ole—eager young man that he was—wanted to make the picnic even more memorable and volunteered to row back to shore to fetch his beloved some ice cream, one of Bess's favorite treats. As he rowed five miles across the lake under a ninety-degree sun, he had a problem. The ice cream was melting. Now Ole was no slouch, but no one could row that fast.

That's when it hit him . . . the idea that would make his name synonymous with the product that he invented, and would eventually bring far-flung reaches of many parts of our country into easy access of millions. He thought to himself, why can't I put an engine on a boat just like the one I built for my horseless carriage? And that's exactly what he did.

It's a little-known fact that the first successful outboard motor was built because a young man in love wanted to bring ice cream to his beloved, who was waiting for him on an island out in the middle of a lake. Remember that the next time you see an outboard motor with the name Ole . . . Evinrude!

About the Author

Little Known Facts is a syndicated radio show featuring true and fascinating facts about how this great country got started. Launched in May 2000, the show is now featured on over 400 stations nationwide. For more information, log on to the Web site at www.littleknownfactsshow.com.

Author Chaz Allen is the creator, producer, and head writer of *Little Known Facts*. A published author, screenwriter, television producer, and radio syndicator, he has always been fascinated with facts and trivia of American life. The popularity of his magazine and newspaper columns through the years was a natural lead-in to creating ths radio show. He is also the author of several bestselling business books and the president of Studio Productions Inc., a leading Southwest production company. He served on the Board of Directors of the National Audio Publishers Association. You may have seen his name as producer on many network television programs over the years. Today he lives in Edmond, Oklahoma and is an avid tennis fan.

Performer Dale Robertson, the voice of *Little Known Facts*, has been one of the world's most beloved and respected celebrities for more than forty-five years. Star of film, television, radio, and stage, he is best known for the famed television series *Tales of Wells Fargo*, *The Iron Horse*, *Death*

Valley Days, and *J.J. Starbuck.* He is also the star of more than sixty-three full-length feature films. His highly acclaimed television roles in *Tales of Wells Fargo* and *Death Valley Days* are on the air somewhere in the world every day.